WORLD GUIDE TO
DOLLS

WORLD GUIDE TO
DOLLS

VALERIE JACKSON DOUET

CHARTWELL
BOOKS, INC.

A QUINTET BOOK

Published by Chartwell Books
A Division of Book Sales, Inc.
110 Enterprise Avenue
Secaucus, New Jersey 07094

ISBN 1-55521-967-5

Creative Director: Richard Dewing
Senior Editor: Laura Sandelson
Designer: Nicky Chapman
Editor: Alison Leach
Photographer: Nick Nicholson

Typeset in Great Britain by
Central Southern Typesetters, Eastbourne
Manufactured in Singapore by Eray Scan Pte Ltd
Printed in Singapore by
Star Standard Industries Pte Ltd

ACKNOWLEDGEMENTS

The author and photographer would like to offer
grateful thanks to the following individuals and
museums for their kind assistance and for allowing us
to photograph dolls in their collections:
Margaret Mundy Whitaker, founder of the Lilliput
Museum Isle of Wight; Beryl Collins; Marion
Jennings; Vivien Greene. Doll artists: Margaret
Glover, Charlotte Zeepvat, Gillie Charlson, Philip
Heath, Vina Cooke, Helene McLeod, Lynn &
Michael Roche; The Abbey House Museum, Leeds;
The Museum of Childhood, Edinburgh; The
Museum of London; Bethnal Green Museum of
Childhood, London; Musée National de Monaco,
Collection de Galea (Mme Bordeau); Musée des
Arts Decoratifs, Paris (Mme Spadeccini Day);
Musée du Jouet, Poissy (Mme Damamme); Museum
Mr Simon van Gijn, Dordrecht; The Collection
Haags Gemeentemuseum, The Hague; Hove
Museum and Art Gallery; The London Toy and
Model Museum; The Museum of Childhood, Judges
Lodgings, Lancaster; The Kirkstall Museum, Leeds;
Tunbridge Wells Museum; Wardown Museum
Luton; Penryhn Castle, Wales; Museum of
Childhood, Ribchester; The National Trust and
Overbecks Museum, Sharpitor, Devon; Warwick
Doll Museum, Castle Museum Arnstadt; The
Spielzug Museum, Sonneberg; Museum of Costume,
Bath; Atelier Wolters van Remmel, The
Netherlands; and all others who wish to remain
anonymous.

Table of Contents

Introduction

The earliest dolls

Dolls are now almost universally regarded as children's toys, though this is a comparatively new concept. The doll form has existed for thousands of years and in the early days of civilization "dolls" were made as ancestor images, idols, fetishes imbued with supernatural powers, fertility symbols, talismen against evil spirits, or sometimes used in rites of magic – the custom of making a wax image of a hated enemy and sticking pins in it to ensure his or her death is well-known even now. Many of these often grotesque and primitive "dolls" are to be found in museums throughout the world, made of every type of material from clay, stone and metal to leaves, beads and twigs.

There were also doll-type funerary images, which replaced the gruesome custom of slaying the wives and servants of departed

BELOW: A woodcut from *Hortis Sanitatis*, 1491, shows a Nuremberg doll-maker at work making dolls with movable limbs.

ABOVE: Greek clay doll, *c*5th century BC, with movable limbs jointed with string. *British Museum.*

BELOW: Early English wooden doll, *c*1770. *Hove Museum.*

VIPs. These were placed in tombs to accompany their master on his journey to the next world and were quite common in Greece, Egypt, Rome, China, Germany and Japan.

It is not possible to say when dolls first became toys for children to play with, but it is known that figures which were clearly dolls, modelled in clay, metal, ivory, bone and other materials, were made in Ancient Greece, where they were dedicated at coming of age ceremonies in the temples. Roman girls also dedicated their dolls to the gods.

The Dark Ages came and went leaving few traces of culture, but there is no doubt that there were toy dolls in Europe by the Middle Ages. Remains of dolls have been found in medieval graves in France and Germany, and doll-makers at work are portrayed in the woodcuts from *Hortus Sanitatis* of 1491. These were mostly made of wood, a material plentiful in the Nuremberg area of Germany, where many dolls originated, but some clay dolls of this period have also been found. Such dolls would have been sold at the numerous saints' day fairs held all over northern Europe. About the same time, in southern Europe, the tradition of making Christmas crib figures of wood and wax flourished.

By the 16th century dolls were being taken to America by the first colonists, as is evident from the famous coloured

ABOVE: Wax-over-composition
bride and groom.

LEFT: Unidentified poured wax
doll, c1880.

BELOW: Glazed china heads,
from Monte Carlo.

drawing by John White in the British Museum, London, of a naked Indian child holding a doll dressed in late Elizabethan dress.

When dolls are described as being wooden wax, papier mâché, bisque or whatever, it does not necessarily mean that they are made of the same substance throughout; a composition doll may have a soft body or a bisque doll a leather one, for example.

Becoming a collector

With such a variety of dolls to choose from, anyone wanting to start a collection must be guided by personal preference and financial considerations. Some people like to concentrate on one type of doll only, for example German bisque or 20th-century cloth, while others choose a particular period, maker or nationality, or try to have some examples of everything. Motives for collecting are also varied; some people collect for investment, others are attracted by the aesthetic qualities of dolls, others by a wish to recapture their childhood.

Having decided which dolls to collect, a course of study will repay the novice collector. Read as many books on the subject as you can find; go to doll fairs, visit museums and attend lectures. Join a doll club, where you can exchange information with other enthusiasts. Establish a rapport with a few dealers (i.e. become a valued customer), who may allow you to handle their dolls. Learn where the makers' marks are hidden. These can be incised, stamped or in relief. If they are on the back of the head, that is a fairly reliable indication of origin. Marks on bodies are not quite so trustworthy, as the body could have been changed. Nor is marked clothing an accurate clue.

In her book *Collecting Dolls* Nora Earnshaw gives a useful summary of where to look for marks. "Bodies that are made of calico, muslin, composition, wood and composition, stockinette and kid may be stamped on the back or on the chest; kid bodies are more often marked on the chest and composition bodies are sometimes stamped or labelled on the side or back. Incised or painted marks may be found on bisque heads at the back of the neck or high on the forehead. Heads of composition, celluloid, wax and wax over another substance may also be marked, although marks on wax should be regarded with suspicion as wax may be scratched so easily. Shoulder-plates of bisque, china, Parian, composition and celluloid may be marked at back or front, while the buttocks of some bisque dolls – those by Schmitt, for instance – may be marked. The soles of the feet of some composition and kid bodies are marked, while many French, British and German manufacturers marked the soles of shoes.

"If you are fortunate to find a doll in its original box, which could be either wood or cardboard, look at the end label: Bru, Jumeau and Stephen Schilling also labelled the underside of the box lid.

"Incised numbers may be found inside bisque, china and Parian arms/hands and on the rim inside the lower leg; such numbers often correspond with size numbers incised on heads and shoulder plates, especially on dolls by Kling or Gaultier."

ABOVE: **Jumeau bisque.**   BELOW: **Parian blond with baby.**

But not all dolls are marked, so other clues to study are found in the style of a doll, in the eyes, in the way the head is made, how the ears and mouth are modelled and how the hair is applied. The maker's style of work is a form of trademark, but it is one that takes a long time to learn.

Dolls may be damaged or they may have been mended so well that the repair is hardly visible, and this is something a collector should appreciate. Look for cracks, undress any doll you intend to buy and examine it carefully. Limbs may be replacements, toes may be missing, ears may be chipped and eyes may have been re-set.

TOP LEFT: Celluloid dolls in national costume.

TOP RIGHT: Modern bisque baby Philip by Heath.

RIGHT: Doll's house servant doll.

FAR RIGHT: Lenci cloth doll.

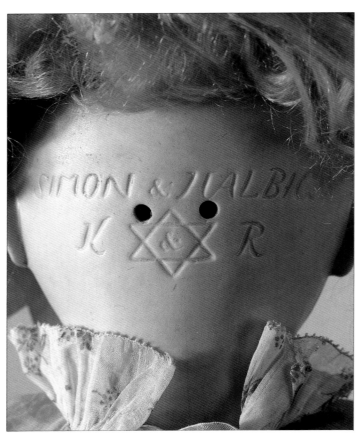

ABOVE: Close up of doll's mark.

Unless it is obviously wrong, clothing is not much of a clue, as old clothes can easily be put on a new doll. Nora Earnshaw says: "If you are offered a fashion doll with the clothes sewn on by modern synthetic thread, check the undergarments. If they are sewn on at all access points (including the bottom of the drawers) by the same thread, the kid body could be a wreck, its condition hidden by the clothes." On the other hand, she points out, it is worth considering buying a badly damaged doll if the clothes are beautiful and original.

Having said all this, if the price of a damaged doll reflects its imperfections and if you like it and want it, then buy it, because the opportunity may never arise again.

Where to buy

Auction sales are a good source of supply, though more suitable for the experienced collector than the beginner, for there are pitfalls. View carefully and remember that the buyer's premium will increase the price by about 15 per cent in most auction houses these days. Fix a price to which you can bid and do not go above it; it is very easy to get carried away by the excitement of the occasion.

Prices of dolls in the auction room vary according to fashion, which, as we all know, is fickle, and to supply and demand. A successful publication about dolls can increase the demand, while the flooding of the market with reproductions can decrease it. There are a great number of dolls currently on the market and if you are buying for investment, it is better to buy a relatively

inexpensive antique doll than a reproduction, however good it is. Other factors influencing the price are the present state of the economy, and the exchange rate between different countries.

Writing in *Dolls* magazine (published in the USA) in Fall 1984, Olivia Bristol of Christie's, South Kensington, reported: "Our clientele doesn't want contemporary dolls . . . In April this year a series of coloured rubber character dolls, all with hats, dating from the 1930s, went for £30 to £40 [$50 to $68] each, as against pre-sale estimates that were double that figure." It is safe to say that as people have begun to know more about recent dolls and to discover their charm and reasonable prices, this attitude has changed considerably.

Doll fairs are a good opportunity for buying, and you may sometimes find dolls at a general antique fair. If you are thinking of starting a collection of more recent dolls, you cannot do better than visit fund-raising events and car boot-sales, where children's cast-off dolls and toys are always to be found among the glassware, unwanted Christmas gifts and all the other fascinating miscellany on display. If you are lucky, you could come across a Norah Wellings velvet cloth doll, or a celluloid one, and there are always plenty of hard plastic and vinyl dolls to be had.

Fakes and reproductions

It is difficult to recognize a good fake, and there are a few about. Even cloth dolls are being reproduced, as well as bisque, china, wooden and wax ones. Some of the points to look for are nylon wigs (old wigs were made of real hair or mohair), new white kid bodies, clothes made of synthetic fabrics and machine-stitched clothing on old fabrics. The first chain-stitch sewing machine was invented in France in 1829 and the sewing machine came into common use in the second half of the 19th century. Hand-stitching, however, is more usual on doll's clothing than machine-stitching, ranging from minute stitches made with a fine needle, to large running stitches.

In their comprehensive *The Collector's Encyclopaedia of Dolls*, D.E. and E. Coleman give some more clues: "Practically all of the bisque heads made today have slip that is relatively free of dirt while kiln dirt is often found in antique heads. Prior to about 1890 most of the French bisque heads were pressed. This was also true in Germany at an earlier date, especially for china heads." They explain that it is more difficult to press a sheet of clay into a mould than it is to pour liquid clay ("slip") into one, so pressed heads can be recognized by their uneven thickness and uneven interior surfaces, while poured heads are smooth.

Check for signs of age, wear and tear on the doll as well as on the clothing – papier mâché and composition dolls wear at the joints. Very white plaster in the eye corners of a bisque doll may mean that the eyes have been replaced.

Become familiar with the makers' marks and where they are situated. Reproduction bisque dolls, made from a mould taken from the original, will show the original manufacturers' marks but the reproduction artist of integrity will put his or her own signature either beneath the existing mark or where it can easily be seen.

Looking after dolls

It is a matter of personal preference how much or how little a doll should be "restored". Some collectors completely re-dress their dolls in modern synthetic fabrics and it has been known for a "crazed" wax-over to be re-dipped in wax, both of which practices are doubtful, to say the least. To quote D.E. and E. Coleman again: "Many dolls have lost their value and charm by re-painting, re-waxing or re-dressing. Extensive repairs transform a doll into a modern imitation of an old doll, no matter how expertly the repairs are done. Of course there are certain repairs that may be necessary, such as replacing a finger, putting a broken head together, replacing a lost eye and so forth. Dolls have had to undergo similar repairs in the past and many of our dolls have heads that were replaced when the original owner broke the head."

A badly smashed head, if it should be replaced, should have a duplicate head of the same vintage. It is not always easy to find such a head, but "replacing a broken antique head or other part of the doll with a modern reproduction is not a valid solution."

The safest course for the amateur is to do as little as possible. If you do intend to try your hand at DIY, practise on a doll of no value and read a book on how to do it first. Careful cleaning can be attempted, though avoid washing papier mâché or wooden dolls, as you can wash away the features.

Try to build up a store of period clothing, which can then be used on an old doll that has none, rather than making a new set that will usually look wrong. The amateur can wash and mend clothing, re-stitch cloth and kid bodies, re-string arms and legs, replace wigs (if possible with mohair or real hair, not nylon) and, if good at modelling, replace a missing finger or toe with one of the many excellent synthetic modelling substances that are now available.

Repairs to wax, wax-over-composition and bisque doll's heads should be left to professionals, who have spent years learning their craft and who know the best materials to use on the dolls and where to get them.

There is not much point in having a collection of beautiful dolls if you have to store them in a box in the attic. Dolls need space and if you have only a limited amount, invest in a glass-fronted cupboard and place it away from both central heating and direct sunlight, which will fade clothing. Wax dolls and dolls with painted surfaces should be kept at a constant temperature and level of humidity.

A doll collection is a valuable asset; keep it secure.

BELOW: **Group of Japanese dolls.**

Wooden Dolls

Wooden dolls or doll forms have been made world-wide since early times. Recognizable doll figures have been found in the Nile Valley preserved by the hot, dry climate of that area. These figures, placed in tombs to serve as a double of the departed or to act as their servants, are among the earliest wooden "dolls" to survive.

Wooden dolls turned on a lathe by woodworkers have also been in existence for many years, and the skittle shape produced by this method is seen again and again, in the dolls of primitive tribes and particularly in the stiff bodies of the 17th- and 18th-century English woodens.

With their painted eyes, red cheeks, prim, painted mouths and beauty spots (a fashion said to have been invented to hide the scars of smallpox), many of the late 17th-century dolls bear a striking resemblance to each other, and to Lady Clapham, the famous doll which, with Lord Clapham, is exhibited in the Victoria & Albert Museum, London. These dolls have a curiously sophisticated, cynical air about them. The head and body were carved from one piece of wood, the head finished with a coat of gesso, the fingers and hands carved and attached to the body with cloth. The legs, too, were carved and set into grooves at the base of the body.

The skittle shape is also seen in the turned wooden dolls of the Ertzgebirge, Germany, and the Sonneberg Museum has several of these, dating to the first part of the 18th century. Some of them are quite large, but many more are small, made as part of the farmyard and market sets sold in boxes, but they all have the same shape. Some of these simple doll figures have arms which move when a string is pulled, so that the bundle in the doll's arms representing a baby, can be rocked.

It is interesting to see this skittle shape recurring in more modern times – for example, in the wooden shoe doll from the Edinburgh Museum of Childhood, which was invented as a plaything for some poor child at the beginning of this century; in the nesting "mother and figure" *matriochkas* dolls from Russia, which have hardly changed at all in style since the 1800s; and in the charming painted *kokeshis* of Japan, made by the woodworkers of the northern mountainous areas who, like their Austrian counterparts, spent the winter carving wooden dolls to amuse the children or to sell at market. Modern versions of the stump doll appear from time to time, made by craftspeople.

All these dolls were overtaken in popularity by the wooden, jointed "Grödnertals", so named after the Groden Valley region in southern Germany where they were made. From the 17th to the 19th century, the Groden region, Bavaria and Thuringia (now known as the Tyrol) were the main areas where woodcarving was practised. The countryside was densely wooded and isolated in winter by the snow, and the peasants would have turned to woodcarving as a pastime as well as a way of augmenting their incomes. There had always been a demand for carved religious figures and it was a natural progression from these to making dolls which could easily be sold by pedlars or at fairs and markets. Nuremberg was the distribution centre for toys of all kinds and by the end of the 19th century wooden dolls from the region were exported all over the world.

It was from here that the penny woodens, the so-called "Dutch" dolls and the peg woodens came, the earlier Grödnertal ones having jointed hips and knees, gesso-covered lower legs and painted slippers. Their short cap of hair was painted, curling gently round the face, and they were made in every possible size from 24in (60cm) to doll's house size or smaller. They came unclothed, which made them ideal playthings, and this was the type of doll Queen Victoria played with as a girl between 1831 and 1833, supervised by her governess, Baroness Lehzen. They are now in the Museum of London. Most of these dolls were dressed as ladies of the nobility and all were given titles by the young princess, while the smaller group represented the famous ballet dancers and opera singers she would have seen at the theatre.

The early Grödnertals degenerated in the latter part of the century, which is not surprising since they were turned out in their hundreds for so much a dozen.

In her book *The Collectors' History of Dolls*, Constance Eileen King distinguishes among the various types of peg doll. It is in the treatment of the head that the greatest differerence between the Grödnertal and the early penny woodens lies. The latter have simple round heads with the hair painted on, whereas the earlier dolls had hairstyles that involved some carving and ornamentation.

These are the best known of the wooden dolls, but folk dolls were made in Sweden, England and Russia as well as in Germany. There are some finely carved Russian dolls, and a carved figure of a woman with a creel and umbrella, with movable head and jaw, dated about 1800, from Rhon, is in the Sonneberg Spielzeugmuseum.

Folk dolls were also made in the USA out of pine wood, which would have been readily available to the early American settlers, but Joel Ellis of Springfield, Vermont, is credited with updating the wooden peg-jointed doll, manufacturing wooden dolls at the Cooperative Manufacturing Co. works in Springfield, Vermont, USA in 1873.

Ellis dolls are rare and expensive and are not often found in Europe. Collectors stand a better chance of finding a Schoenhut doll at a more reasonable price because they were exported to France, Germany and Britain. Albert Schoenhut was born in 1850 and went to the USA when he was 17. He invented a successful toy piano in 1872 which launched him on his career as a toy-maker. The subsequent Humpty Dumpty circus, which came complete with animals and performers, was another success, and in 1911 Schoenhut patented his first design for a wooden doll.

The Schoenhut dolls are complicated pieces of work, with a mechanism of steel spring hinges, double-spring tension and swivel connections. The dolls – girls, boys and babies – could be placed in natural positions. They were made entirely of wood, with no rubber cord, painted with enamel oil colours and stood firmly on posts which fitted into the soles of the feet and on to a metal disc. The dolls had carved and painted hair, some with ribbons and hats; some had painted eyes, others glass eyes. They came in 60 different styles. There was even a wooden Bye-Lo Baby, patterned on Grace Storey Putnam's successful doll, but it was not marketed because of copyright problems.

The All Wood Perfection Art Dolls were an instant success and they deserved to be, for they were sturdy, aesthetically pleasing (the heads were carved by Graziano, one of the best-known sculptors of the time) and attractively dressed. About 1911 the most expensive Schoenhut dolls, 21in (52cm) high, sold at $90 (£53) per dozen wholesale which, when you add the retailer's mark-up, was not cheap at the time. After Albert's death in 1912 the firm was continued by his sons, who ran it successfully until 1934, when it became bankrupt. It rose once more from the ashes to continue making some of its lines but again went into bankruptcy in the 1940s.

Since the invention of plastics and vinyl, few firms bother to produce wooden dolls and in the latter part of the 20th century it is left to a few artist craftspeople to continue this tradition. The Swiss and German husband-and-wife team of Abhinavo and Regina Sandreuter have created superb wooden models of children with articulated bodies made of eight wooden parts joined by elastic string held by wooden dowels. The heads and limbs are modelled in clay by the artists, then cast and mechanically produced in maple wood, the fine detail of each doll being hand-carved by the artists. The results are exquisite.

In France, some charming lacquered wood characters from *The Adventures of Tintin*, made in 1986, were exhibited at the Musée des Poupées, Josselin (Rohan Collection), while in England Lynne and Michael Roche are making high quality dolls with porcelain heads and hands and turned, jointed, poseable wooden bodies.

Caring for wooden dolls

The humidity level of storage for wooden dolls is very important because wood expands when it absorbs moisture and contracts when it is dry, which can lead to cracking.

Many wooden dolls are covered with gesso and then painted and varnished. They should therefore not be washed unless it is essential, and then only after first using neutral soap on a clean soft cloth on an inconspicuous part. If the paint or varnish starts to lift, stop cleaning. The main point to remember is to avoid soaking the doll with water.

Collecting wooden dolls

One only has to look at the prices achieved at some of the recent auction sales of early wooden dolls to realize that they are out of reach of the ordinary collector. Schoenhut dolls, however, are more reasonably priced for the serious enthusiast and 19th-century peg woodens can still be found among the less expensive dolls. However, the discerning collector could hardly do better than invest in one of the fine wooden dolls being made today.

1 THURINGIAN TURNED DOLLS

Three nursing dolls in painted, turned wood with movable arms. When the string is pulled, the arms move up and down, rocking the baby.

The blue doll is a copy of an old Sonneberg design, but the others are original and probably came from Viechtau, south of Sonneberg.

The skittle shape is made by turning the dolls on a lathe, a technique also seen on smaller dolls which were part of the matchwood boxed sets sold in the 18th century. These included farms, a hunt, a park, a fair, a zoo, an ark and many other brightly coloured scenes from everyday life, all fitting neatly into a box.

DATE
18th century
NATIONALITY
German
AVAILABILITY
rare, expensive
HEIGHT
approx 9in (23cm)

2 RUSSIAN CARVED DOLLS

These two carved and painted dolls, an officer and his lady, are said to be Russian, though they could have originated in Germany.

Oberammergau figures, similar to these, stand on a carved base and were frequently used as domestic ornaments in place of porcelain, putting them rather on the fringe of the doll world, but they are none the less attractive and are clearly the work of a skilled carver.

The lady is wearing a smart hat with streamers and is holding a small dog beneath her cloak, on which the trimming is skilfully indicated by strokes of the chisel. The officer wears a shako and a frogged jacket with epaulettes – a Hussar perhaps? He is carrying a baton and wearing a sword.

DATE
c1800
NATIONALITY
probably German
AVAILABILITY
rare, expensive
HEIGHT
13¾in (35cm)

3 OAK DOLL

The oldest doll in the collection of the Abbey House Museum, Leeds, UK, this carved oak figure is holding a bottle and glass.

Found in a Yorkshire farmhouse that was being demolished, it is one of several dolls donated by the late Kenneth Sanderson, a keen collector in the 1940s and 1950s.

As can be seen, this figure was not turned on a lathe but was carved directly out of a piece of oak. It was probably made by a carpenter at the end of a building job, from wood left over from his work, to amuse a child.

DATE
17th century
NATIONALITY
English
AVAILABILITY
rare, expensive
HEIGHT
approx 9in (23cm)

4 SHOE DOLL

One of an unusual group of dolls from the Edward Lovett collection in the Edinburgh Museum of Childhood.

It is what the collector called an "emergency" or improvised doll, a plaything for an unfortunate child whose parents could not afford a shop doll and who made one out of waste materials such as the sole of a shoe (like the doll seen here), or a clay pipe, paper and rags or sometimes even a mutton bone.

About the turn of the century, Edward Lovett used to walk round the streets exchanging shop dolls for these pathetic scraps, and he acquired this particular doll in a London slum about 1905. It is touching to see how an attempt has been made to give the doll a face of coarse nails and arms and legs of sticks bound with rags.

DATE
1905
NATIONALITY
English
AVAILABILITY
rare, expensive
HEIGHT
12in (30cm)

4

6

5 MODERN STUMP DOLLS

Four turned and painted stump dolls by Robin and Nell Dale who work from their farmhouse in Lancashire, UK. They are members of the British Toymakers Guild.

Designers and makers of all kinds of turned and hand-painted wooden figures and chess sets in the traditional English style, the Dales make a variety of these figures.

Here you see a butcher, a policeman, a chef and a farmer's wife, but they also make a colourful set of *Alice Through the Looking Glass* chess figures and a great many other characters. The Dales's beautifully designed and finished stump dolls are so called because in the 18th century they were made from stumps of wood.

DATE
late 20th century
NATIONALITY
English
AVAILABILITY
easy to find, inexpensive
HEIGHT
8in (20cm)

6 LATE PEG WOODEN DOLL

A typical wooden top doll, with a less shapely (but fully jointed) body than the Grödnertals, a skittle-shaped head and a nose in sharp relief.

The face is fairly crude, with red cheeks and roughly painted features. The hands and feets are knobs. The hair is a plain black cap, with no face curls, though some attempt has been made to add a few extra curls on top of the painted cap.

This particular doll has been finely dressed in clothes that appear to be in the fashion of the late 19th century, but they are not original. It is quite a large doll, giving more scope for ornate fabric and trimmings than is possible on a small one.

DATE
c1870
NATIONALITY
German
AVAILABILITY
easy to find inexpensive
HEIGHT
22in (56cm)

5

7 ERIC HORNE PEG DOLLS

Eric Horne and his son, Peter, are craftsmen who make traditional jointed wooden peg dolls. Their studio in Exeter, UK, is equipped like a mini-factory with lathe, bandsaw, planing bench and assembly room. The jointed beechwood dolls range from 18in (46cm) to the tiny ¼in (6mm) size that is sold either inside a wooden egg or in a perspex box with a magnifying glass on top so that you can inspect the fine workmanship.

All the dolls, except the two smallest sizes, are fully jointed and pegged with wooden pins; the two smallest are jointed at the shoulders and thighs. The bodies are all turned on the lathe; legs and heads are painted with undercoat, sanded and then repainted with non-toxic enamels, so their finish is greatly superior to that of the traditional peg dolls.

DATE
20th century
NATIONALITY
English
AVAILABILITY
easy to find, inexpensive
HEIGHT
8½in (21.5cm)

8 GRÖDNERTAL DOLL

This peg-jointed wooden Grödnertal doll has black painted hair with curls framing the face, which was the height of fashion from about 1800 to 1820. A famous painting of 1805 by François Gérard shows Madame Récamier with just such a hairstyle and also with a low-cut dress much like that seen on this doll, though perhaps the doll's dress is more modest. The puffed sleeves are typical of the time, too.

The face and neck are delicately painted then varnished, and the doll has carved ears from which hang ear drops.

She wears flat red slippers and a smart feathered bonnet.

DATE
c1815
NATIONALITY
German
AVAILABILITY
rare, expensive
HEIGHT
12in (30cm)

8

7

9 GRÖDNERTAL DOLL II

It is interesting to compare this doll with the modern peg version by Eric Horne. Here we have the ball and socket joints which were an innovation introduced by Heinrich Stier of Sonneberg – joints that had long been used in lay-figures for artists. The head is in the traditional early manner, with two tones of hair and curls framing the face and a carved comb on the head, which was usually painted yellow. Such dolls have been named tuck comb dolls by collectors.

The dolls come in a range of sizes from 6in (15cm) to 24in (60cm), and they were made, with variations, for 50 years, which makes it difficult to date them accurately.

DATE
c1810
NATIONALITY
German
AVAILABILITY
rare, expensive
HEIGHT
16in (41cm)

10 GIRL WITH BONNET

This wooden doll, which is in excellent condition, has all the hallmarks of the mid-18th century English woodens. Her face is of painted and varnished gesso on a wood ground, and her dark glass eyes are surrounded by painted, stitch-like eyelashes and eyebrows. Her hair is nailed on and she has no feet. Her legs are jointed at the hip, and her arms and hands are made of kid leather.

Her clothes, which are finely sewn with tiny hems and tucks, are original and she also possesses another, working dress of blue and white gingham.

DATE	mid-18th century
NATIONALITY	English
AVAILABILITY	rare, expensive
HEIGHT	12in (30cm)

11 SCOTTISH WOODEN DOLL

A young girl in a gown with leading strings hanging down her back. These do not necessarily mean that the doll is supposed to represent a child, as they were worn by all dependent females at that time. The doll has broad shoulders and hips and a narrow waist, as was the fashion.

Her silken arms are attached with wire to carved wooden forearms and hands, and her wooden legs are peg-jointed at the hips and knees.

Her green silk dress is laced up at the back and she wears a full skirt over a quilted pink silk petticoat and a quilted cap.

DATE	mid-18th century
NATIONALITY	English
AVAILABILITY	rare, expensive
HEIGHT	20in (51cm)

11

10

12 FAMILY GROUP

A delightful family of three dolls, though their relationship is unclear, as the lady doll is wearing the leading strings that usually denoted single status. The dolls have the fixed dark glass eyes of the mid-18th century, the brushstroke eyebrows above a single line and the prim mouth seen in others of this type. The gesso-coated faces and the hair must have been restored.

The boy is wearing a collarless coat finished off with a cravat at the neck, knee breeches with stockings and buckled leather shoes.

DATE	18th century
NATIONALITY	English
AVAILABILITY	rare, expensive
HEIGHT	tallest doll 19in (48cm)

The girl on the left has the fashionable narrow waist and is wearing a dress with three-quarter length sleeves from which emerge chemise sleeves trimmed with lace. It was fashionable to match the sleeve lace with that on the cap and on the edge of the bodice, so the dolls come from a family of means.

12

13 ROUNDED FOREHEAD DOLL

 This doll with a high bosom and a rounded forehead has her hair swept back under a "pinner" or lace-trimmed cap. Her well-painted face has dark glass eyes, with painted stitch-like eyelashes and eyebrows. She is wearing smart red earrings in her nicely carved ears.

The low neck of her dress is filled with a lace "tucker" for modesty, which matches the lace of her cap. The dress has a pointed stomacher over the full skirt and loose, three-quarter length sleeves with lace chemise-sleeves emerging from them. The skirt is open to show a quilted petticoat and under her skirt she is wearing long blue stockings and slippers with white leather soles. On her hands she is wearing leather mittens.

DATE	*1740s*
NATIONALITY	*English*
AVAILABILITY	*rare, expensive*
HEIGHT	*20in (51cm)*

13

14

14 WOODEN DOLL

 This doll dating from 1800 is not quite as finely made as the previous one. She has a more child-like body and long arms, which stretch to the shoulder rather than to the elbows.

She is dressed in a high-waisted cotton smock in the fashion of the Regency, a style that would have been worn by the ladies of Jane Austen's time. She also possesses a green bonnet, though here you see her without it, her blond lambswool ringlets are trimmed with blue ribbon, then sewn to a calico cap which was nailed to the head.

DATE	*c1800*
NATIONALITY	*English*
AVAILABILITY	*rare, expensive*
HEIGHT	*19in (48cm)*

Beneath the smock is an older style bodice and a linen slip, suggesting that the doll was re-dressed after she was made.

15 DOLL WITH POMANDER

This lovely doll, dated about 1725, was given to the Lilliput Museum, Isle of Wight, by the family that had owned her for 250 years. Her head and body are carved from one piece of wood and her legs are jointed. The arms are joined to the body by a strip of fabric.

She is wearing a green cap under her bonnet and a low-cut bodice, which is modestly filled with a neckerchief. An apron covers the front of her dress and she is quite plainly dressed – perhaps she is one of the lower classes.

The visible parts of the body are painted in gesso and enamel, and the eyes have no pupils and are made of dark glass, outlined in painted dots. The hair is real, and the clothes are original.

The doll carries a woven basket ball which represents a herb-filled pomander, carried to overcome the smells of the streets and in the hope of warding off disease.

DATE
c1725
NATIONALITY
English
AVAILABILITY
rare, expensive
HEIGHT
20in (51cm)

16 PIANO DOLLS

Also known as Bristle dolls, these charming little figures are only 2½in (6cm) high. Their bodies are supported by four bristles, and when they are placed on a piano and it vibrates, their hanging, articulated legs "dance".

Sometimes these dolls were made of moulded dough or composition. Another variation was a doll with a bunch of bristles hidden beneath a skirt, which would move when the vibration started.

They were a very simple form of walking doll.

DATE
mid-19th century
NATIONALITY
German
AVAILABILITY
rare, inexpensive
HEIGHT
2½in (6cm)

17 FRENCH WOODEN DOLL

The Musée National de Monaco contains the Galéa collection of dolls, automata and accessories, representing Madeleine de Galéa's passionate interest in the beauty of dolls and their clothes in the first part of the century.

The dolls are mainly elegantly attired lady dolls dating back to the 18th century, with the addition of some automata.

This beautiful 18th-century doll from the Galéa collection wears a silk dress decorated with blue flowers in the Sacque fashion, a comfortable garment with small box pleats behind falling from the neck and merging into the folds of the gown below the shoulders, a type of dress often seen in paintings by Watteau. The three-quarter sleeves are trimmed with deep lace.

The face of the doll is beautifully carved, coated with gesso and painted; note the delicately moulded eyelids. The hands, too, are finely shaped and finished. The doll has no legs but is resting on a cone-shaped support.

DATE
18th century
NATIONALITY
French
AVAILABILITY
rare, expensive
HEIGHT
33in (84cm)

17

18 FRENCH WOODEN DOLL

A large wooden doll, with articulated ball and socket joints and hooks on her knees to keep them straight. Her face and hair are painted on a gesso ground, and she is wearing a copy of her original costume, which was so badly damaged that it could not be used. She was given to the Musée des Arts Décoratifs in 1909. The doll could easily be French, though the hair is painted in the style of the early German wooden dolls.

DATE
c1810
NATIONALITY
probably French
AVAILABILITY
rare, expensive
HEIGHT
30½in (77cm)

18

19 & 20 PEDLAR DOLLS

DATE
1790
NATIONALITY
English
AVAILABILITY
rare, expensive
HEIGHT
9½in (24cm)

These delightful wooden pedlar dolls probably date from about 1790. Such dolls were very popular in the 18th and 19th centuries. Their costumes are typical of the clothes which would have been worn by itinerant pedlars of the day. The woman wears a neat bonnet and dress with a crossed neckerchief. (In winter, she would have worn a warm cloak under which she sheltered her basket.)

The man, a very dashing fellow, looks as if he has been in the navy and there is a naval connection, for these dolls are thought to have been sold by pedlars in Portsmouth, UK.

The dolls were made by C. & H. White of Milton, Portsmouth, which made many such figures. Another pair is in the Bethnal Green Museum of Childhood, London, but the items sold are different. Though they are probably basically made of wood, the faces, hands and feet are covered with white kid leather, which probably accounts for their name of chicken skin pedlars. Their eyes are black beads.

It is interesting to see the goods they are selling and the detail here is amazing. The lady pedlar is holding a candlestick and on her tray are nutmeg graters, pomanders, a book of "curiosities", another of Old Ballads and another of English poems, as well as spools of thread, laces for stays and lengths of lace.

The man is carrying "cold cream" in a little box, "Packwood's patent balsam syrup", "roseate bloom", "pearl powder", fancy braces for the gentlemen, beads, buttons and packets of paper.

In the 18th and 19th centuries pedlars provided an essential service to isolated communities, selling things that would be unobtainable except in large towns and bringing a touch of urban sophistication to rural lives.

21 STALL HOLDER

This stall holder with painted wooden head and glass eyes is said to date from about 1830, but in her patterned dress, cap and neckerchief she bears a striking resemblance to some of the early English wooden dolls of the previous century.

On the stall is an assortment of domestic objects for sale, including a knife sharpener, a tray, brushes and mops. Not seen in this photograph are a pair of pattens which were worn over shoes to keep indoor footwear out of the mud.

DATE
probably 18th century
NATIONALITY
Dutch
AVAILABILITY
rare, expensive
HEIGHT
6¾in (17cm)

22 CRÈCHE FIGURES

Four painted wooden crèche figures on stands, dating from the beginning of the 19th century. They are part of a larger group.

Crèche figures were made by artists and craftsmen for religious purposes, which accounts for the high standard of carving and finish. Sometimes the figures had inset glass eyes, though here they are painted, and all the figures have wigs.

Many crèche groups were made in Italy, where they would have been displayed in churches, houses and palaces at Christmas. The groups included extras such as bystanders, portraits of the family who had ordered the scene to be made, villagers, birds and animals, as well as the Holy Family.

DATE
early 19th century
NATIONALITY
German or Italian
AVAILABILITY
rare, expensive
HEIGHT
17–23in (43–58cm)

The facts that these figures are made in wood rather than terracotta or wax and that they have applied hair, as well as their slightly stiff bearing and style of clothing, suggest that they may have been made in Bavaria or Austria, with its long tradition of wood carving.

23 MAN DOLL

This rare 18th-century doll is dressed *à la Française*, which would have been the correct clothing for a man of high social standing at that time.

The broad cuffs, cravat, wide-skirted and waisted jacket, tricorne hat and long waistcoat date it to the second quarter of of the century.

His head, lower arms, hands and lower legs are made of wood, coated with gesso, while the body, upper arms and legs are of stuffed fabric. He has real hair and painted eyes.

It is interesting to note that Lord Clapham, the famous early 18th-century doll who, with Lady Clapham, resides in the Victoria & Albert Museum, in London, wears just such a red coat, a fashion introduced in the 1660s.

DATE
second quarter of 18th century
NATIONALITY
Dutch
AVAILABILITY
rare, expensive
HEIGHT
16½in (42cm)

24 ALMUT AUGUSTINE

The late Almut Augustine (died 1992) was a talented German maker of wooden dolls who lived to the south of Nuremberg. Trained as a kindergarten teacher, she began making dolls at the age of 17. Some of them had soft bodies, but this one, which is a self-portrait of the maker as a child and which she exhibited just before she died, is entirely of wood. Almut Augustine worked in lime wood, a large supply of which she purchased 25 years ago when the lime trees in her road were chopped down.

The hair she used on her dolls was real baby hair, given to her by neighbours when they cut their children's hair and kept carefully for future use.

DATE
1990s
NATIONALITY
German
AVAILABILITY
rare, expensive
HEIGHT
approx 14in (36cm)

25 SCHOENHUT GIRL DOLL

All-wood dolls were made by the American firm of Schoenhut from 1911 to 1926. They were fully jointed at the neck, shoulders and elbows, wrists, hips, knees and ankles. They were joined together with steel spring hinges and swivel connections, so it is not surprising that so many have survived, even though they may have lost some of their surface paint.

The heads were modelled of solid basswood, carved by the Italian Graziano, who was one of the best known sculptors of that time. They had either carved hair or mohair wigs; human hair was never used. The dolls were painted with natural oil colours, so they could be cleaned. Toy shops sold separate outfits for them. This girl doll, with her wooden hair and eager expression, shows how attractive they were. She is not wearing her original dress or shoes.

DATE
c1914
NATIONALITY
American
AVAILABILITY
easy to find, mid-price range
HEIGHT
16in (41cm)

26 SCHOENHUT GIRL DOLL II

Another type of Schoenhut wooden doll, also fully jointed and with a head modelled of solid basswood. This doll has painted hair and a bonnet which is carved in with the head. It has intaglio eyes.

It is just one of the many designs of doll made by the firm, for there were boys as well as girls, some had ribbons and caps, others had set-in glass eyes, and they came in four sizes.

The clothing for the dolls was of the style of the time, some elaborate and expensive, other garments less so, but all reflected what children wore at that period in the USA. This particular doll has been re-dressed. It would have been bought wearing a one-piece, lace-trimmed garment that reached the knees.

Albert Schoenhut died at the age of 63 in 1912, and his six sons continued to operate the business, bringing out new designs, among which was a walking doll. The first Schoenhut company ran until 1934.

DATE
c1914
NATIONALITY
American
AVAILABILITY
easy to find, mid-price range
HEIGHT
16in (41cm)

26

27 DOOR OF HOPE BRIDE

A mission called the Door of Hope was founded in Shanghai in 1901 to save children, slave girls and young widows from destitution. The girls were taught to sew and embroider, and they used these skills on the Door of Hope dolls, for which they received payment. The mission was closed after World War II. There was a similar mission in Canton.

The heads, arms and hands were made of carved wood by a local woodcarver and the dolls were so smooth that they did not have to be painted, though the lips, hair and eyes were coloured. The bodies were of stuffed cloth.

DATE
1920–30
NATIONALITY
Chinese
AVAILABILITY
rare, expensive
HEIGHT
11in (28cm) and 11½in (29cm)

This Door of Hope bride is wearing a red coat embroidered with gold and her feet are bound. The groom wears a black silk outfit; his hair is in a bun.

28 JOEL ELLIS DOLL

This rare doll may not be very beautiful but it is extremely interesting. Made by the Cooperative Doll Co., *c*1873, it has a wooden head and body and metal hands and feet, which are encased in boots. It is jointed at the neck, shoulders, elbows, hips and knees by mortise and tenon jointing.

The Cooperative Doll Co. of Springfield, Vermont, USA, manufactured wooden dolls patented by Joel Ellis, employing about 60 people. The wooden heads were roughly cut, then steamed, softened and pressed into a head shape. The body and limbs were turned on a lathe.

DATE
c1873
NATIONALITY
American
AVAILABILITY
rare, expensive
HEIGHT
12in (30cm)

Wax Dolls

Wax is an excellent modelling material, giving a smooth and attractive translucent effect which cannot be achieved in any other medium. It has long been used for making life-sized portraits or effigies. The 16th-century Italian craftsman, Cellini, made replicas of deceased noble persons for display in churches and chapels. Even in England there are two life-sized models in wax of Katherine, Duchess of Buckingham (died 1743) and her son, the Marquess of Normandy, in Westminster Abbey, by an unknown artist. Crèche figures were also made, as were wax relief portraits, which were fashionable in the 18th and 19th centuries, when they were hung in the drawing rooms of upper- and middle-class homes.

As wax is such an easily worked and readily obtainable material, as well as having such an attractive, smooth finish, it was an obvious choice for doll-making. Some very early small wax dolls are still in existence in the old doll's houses in the Rijksmuseum, Amsterdam, in the Haags Gemeentemuseum, The Hague, in the Frans Halsmuseum, Haarlem, the Netherlands, in the German National-museum, Nuremberg, and in the wonderful series of 18th-century doll's rooms at Arnstadt, Germany, known as "Mon Plaisir".

Although wax is such a malleable material and agreeable to work with, it does have the disadvantage of being easily destructible. One hears many sad tales of wax dolls being left out in the sun for too long by careless young owners. Heat is the number one enemy, and owners of wax dolls have to be careful not to store them near direct heating.

Because of their vulnerability, few very early wax dolls exist, though the Bethnal Green Museum of Childhood, London, does have the 8in (20cm) 1754 wax doll that belonged to Laetitia Clark. She married a Powell and started the family tradition of dressing dolls in the fashion of the day, so that there is a series of 44 of these dolls from 1754 to 1910.

A distinction has to be made here between poured wax dolls and wax-over-papier mâché or wax-over-composition dolls. The poured wax method was to make a mould of a clay head and lower limbs, then to pour tinted, heated wax into the mould. When a thick shell had been formed after one or more pourings, the excess was drained off. Legs and arms would be almost solid, the head thick enough to with-stand a certain amount of handling.

In the wax-over-papier mâché or composition technique, the doll was dipped in wax once or twice to give it a finer finish. Both techniques developed concurrently in the 19th century.

The English were the undoubted leaders of the poured wax doll industry in the 19th century. Skilled artists such as Herbert Meech, Lucy Peck, Charles Marsh and John Edwards were working at about the same time as the Italian families of Montanari, who had settled in London at the beginning of the 19th century, and Pierotti, who had established themselves in the previous century. The dolls were sold by agents or in shops and bazaars and many found their way to the USA, where they could be purchased by the mid-1800s. By the 1870s there were wax dolls in profusion, with turning heads, pierced ears, composition arms and legs and also wax-over-papier mâché dolls, all exported by firms with an eye for a new market.

It is difficult to identify the dolls made by a particular maker unless they are marked with the maker's mark. Fortunately, many are stamped on the stuffed body, though only rarely signed. Some Pierotti dolls have the name scratched on the back of the head — but even that is not reliable proof of identification, for wax is easily scratched.

Most wax dolls had stuffed calico bodies, on which the lower arms and legs were added, and a wax shoulder-plate that fitted over the torso, all taped through holes and securely tied.

Some dolls had a fringe of hair on a braid strip, which was wound round the head, others had hair inserted into a central slit in the head, but the finest dolls all had real hair, eyebrows and lashes inserted into the wax singly or in groups. The technique of inserting hair differed slightly from doll-maker to doll-maker, but they all used a sort of metal tool to cut the wax head and a heated tool to seal in the hair again. It was a laborious process. Sometimes a doll-maker would offer to use a child's hair on her own doll.

Wax-over-composition

Poured wax dolls are expensive but those of wax-over-papier mâché or composition are less so and examples can be found at low prices if they are not in pristine condition. Some of the slit-headed and pumpkin-headed dolls are very attractive but the disadvantage of any wax-over doll is that they often have "crazed" faces, due to the expansion and contraction of the substance under the wax, and not a great deal can be done about this, even by a skilled restorer.

Slit-heads are so named because the hair is inserted into a slit running from crown to forehead and allowed to fall in ringlets at the side of the face. Those made before 1850 have dark glass eyes without pupils. Bodies, legs and feet are stuffed, the arms are often of leather and they all seem to wear an enigmatic smile, as if in possession of a nice secret they are keeping to themselves.

Pumpkin-headed dolls have fancy moulded hairstyles, stuffed bodies, wooden limbs and black, pupil-less eyes. Another type of wax-over-papier mâché is the bonnet head, wearing a moulded hat but with the same staring, dark eyes.

Caring for wax dolls

Wax is strong enough to withstand the gentle warmth of a room but not hot sun or other direct source of heat. Direct sunlight should in any case be avoided because colours will fade where exposed and it is almost impossible to match the original colour of a wax doll. In *The History of Wax Dolls* Mary Hillier writes: "Most old dolls will benefit from a careful spring clean. But take care not to touch the actual fabric of the wax. Beyond that, it is always more desirable to call in the help of a professional wax restorer."

In her book *Collecting Dolls* Nora Earnshaw has this sound advice to give about caring for wax dolls:

"Keep wax dolls away from strong lights in cabinets and inspect their bodies periodically, especially at the point where the shoulder is attached to the body; the glue hardens with age and the calico could rot as the hardened glue contracts. If the face of a wax doll is very grimy, do not, repeat not, put moisture anywhere near the head or limbs; this applies also to wax-over-papier mâché dolls. Take up a very little cold cream on a soft, smooth white cloth, and gently wipe the doll's face. Be especially careful not to go too close to the painted features – the eyebrows, crease of the eyelid and around the mouth. Keep turning the cloth as you go – wipe and clean, wipe and clean – and make sure you have wiped away every trace of residual cold cream; you will be very pleased with the result.

"Never put a plastic bag immediately next to wax as condensation will affect the texture of the wax. White or natural pure silk or fine white lawn are the safest fabrics to place next to any type of doll."

Collecting wax dolls

Top quality poured wax dolls are expensive to buy, the price being affected by the condition of the doll, whether it has been restored (and if so, how well) and the condition of the clothing. Wax-over-composition dolls are less expensive.

In her book *The Collectors' History of Dolls* Constance Eileen King writes: "When buying wax dolls, some degree of damage has to be accepted, as absolutely perfect wax dolls are rare. A doll with limbs that are slightly damaged is far preferable to one with replaced parts, though some restoration, if well done, helps the doll retain a pleasing effect. Wax does sometimes fade, so suspicion should not necessarily be aroused by a doll whose legs differ slightly in colour from the shoulder head, if it has been exposed to the light for many years; though if the colour is very different, the cord sewing on the legs should be compared to that fixing other wax parts, and the suspect limbs should be examined for a too-pristine condition . . . It is better to accept a crack that runs down the face than to attempt a restoration that is likely to prove unsuccessful, as poured-wax dolls, once fractured through, will always show the crack."

1 PIEROTTI BABY

This mid-19th century poured wax Pierotti baby has its head slightly turned to one side and the delicate features are typical of the work of this family of doll-makers. The baby is wearing a tucked and trimmed pelisse and and ruched bonnet, which are original – if a doll was large enough, it could be dressed in real baby clothes. The bent-limbed body is made of stuffed cloth, but the lower limbs are made of wax.

The baby doll developed gradually during the 19th century but was not mass-produced until Edwardian times; before that time dolls were depicted as miniature adults, and children were regarded in the same way.

The baby has inset eyebrows, lashes and hair and is a fine example of its kind.

DATE
c1885
NATIONALITY
English
AVAILABILITY
rare, expensive
HEIGHT
20in (51cm)

2 MONTANARI DOLL

A fine example of a Montanari wax doll, with wax lower limbs attached with eyelets, and a soft body. Her hair is inserted and her eyes are fixed. The presence of teeth on a doll of this type is unusual. The little creases of fat on the neck and at the wrists give a delightful impression of childhood, and the doll has such character that it is very likely that it was modelled on a real child.

She is wearing her original clothing which is complete down to the lace-trimmed drawers, flannel petticoat and all the other usual Victorian underwear.

DATE
1880
NATIONALITY
English
AVAILABILITY
rare, expensive
HEIGHT
28in (71cm)

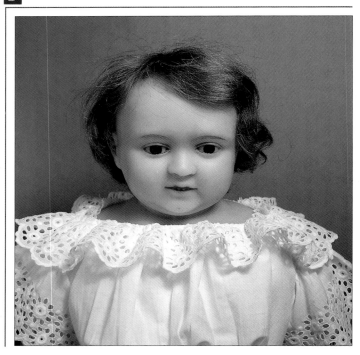

3

3 PIEROTTI BABY II

This doll is attributed to Pierotti, and it certainly bears a strong resemblance to the doll above The colours have faded considerably over the years. The doll's wax legs and feet, which have always been covered up, are a perfect pink.

The doll has inserted eyelashes and eyebrows, blue eyes and blonde hair. It has a stamp on its body: "Hamley's Regent Street Doll Emporium." It is fully clothed, right down to its flannel petticoat, and has an elaborate bonnet trimmed with ruching and lace and a tucked dress.

DATE
c1865
NATIONALITY
English
AVAILABILITY
rare, expensive
HEIGHT
12in (30cm)

4 LARGE POURED WAX DOLL

This large poured wax doll may have been a shop model. Many wax models were made for fashion shops at the end of the 19th century.

The doll is attributed to the Marsh family, which specialized in life-sized children, and it is dated about 1890. The chubby, well-rounded limbs, direct gaze and rather English looks are typical of the work of Charles Marsh, as is the beautiful modelling.

The doll has inset eyebrows and lashes. Her rather pale colouring may be due to the wax having faded in a shop window.

DATE	*c1890*
NATIONALITY	*English*
AVAILABILITY	*rare, expensive*
HEIGHT	*38½in (98cm)*

5

5 PRINCESS LOUISE AS A BRIDE

Vivien Greene says: "The underwear of the doll is exquisite; the drawers have a deep flounce of Chantilly lace and a knot of blue satin ribbon is caught up at the side . . . The first petticoat is elaborately embroidered cream nun's veiling, the silk petticoat barred with narrow cream satin and lace and the skirt itself is ivory satin with guipure lace around the hem and train . . . The stockings are cream openwork silk, with disproportionately small white kid shoes."

Vivien Greene was left this doll, a portrait of Princess Louise, granddaughter of Queen Victoria, by a friend. It is by Lucy Peck and it shows the Princess as she was at the age of 22, dressed in her wedding finery.

Her marriage to the Duke of Fife took place in 1887, but this doll was made a little later than that.

DATE	*c1887*
NATIONALITY	*English*
AVAILABILITY	*rare, expensive*
HEIGHT	*approx 24in (61cm)*

6 MEECH DOLLS

Two dolls by the Meech family. One of them bears the stamped trademark of Meech on one thigh. She is wearing a red velvet beret which matches the cherry-coloured ribbon trimming of her dress. Her companion wears a later homemade dress. Both the dolls have soft brown human hair set in the wax crown and the rather dismal expression of many Meech dolls. It is thought that they may have been modelled on one of Herbert Meech's own daughters.

Meech started his career in Madame Tussaud's waxworks when he was about 16 years old. By the time he was 19 in 1852 he had started his own factory in Kennington, London. Three of his children worked for him, and one of them, Ernest, carried on the business into the 1920s.

DATE	*c1880*
NATIONALITY	*English*
AVAILABILITY	*rare, expensive*
HEIGHT	*26in (66cm)*

6

7 MONTANARI DOLL

DATE
c1860

NATIONALITY
English

AVAILABILITY
rare, expensive

HEIGHT
31in (79cm)

Amy is dressed in the authentic mourning dress of a three-year-old child of the 19th century, reflecting a period of high mortality in which many children spent much of their young lives dressed in black.

Mrs Greene quotes from *A Manual of Domestic Economy, suited to families spending from £100 to £1000 a year:* "It may, however, be stated as certainly three hundred to one against a death occurring (i.e in childbirth) in any young woman of fair average health, who is well formed, and who will have the advantage of good nursing, and a mind free from care. In those who are not so favourably situated, the mortality is increased to one percent."

At first Vivien Greene dressed the doll in a Victorian tucked and embroidered white cambric dress to cheer her up, but later it became clear that the original black dress, with folded crêpe at sleeves and neckline, was the historically correct wear and Amy seemed more herself in it.

Her arms and legs are fragile, as they are hollow poured wax, attached to the cloth body by metal eyelets. Underneath her dress she wears a linen chemise, cambric drawers and one petticoat trimmed with heavy handmade lace edging. Her feet are beautifully moulded, with tiny toenails. Her pale face, with softly coloured mouth and deep blue eyes with dark lashes, has a sad expression as befits a mourning doll.

8 JOHN EDWARDS CRYING DOLL

John Edwards worked in London from 1868 to 1907. He made dolls for Queen Victoria and exhibited at the London Exhibition in 1871.

This rare crying baby doll has a slightly pink face, with an open mouth showing its tongue. The eyes with lashes are closed, and the doll has blond real hair and a cloth body with poured wax lower limbs.

It is wearing a long lace-panelled, pin-tucked christening robe and a cut silk cream bonnet decorated with lace.

The realism of the crying face indicates that Edwards modelled this baby from life.

DATE
c1870

NATIONALITY
English

AVAILABILITY
rare, expensive

HEIGHT
19½in (49.5cm)

His three daughters would have given him plenty of opportunity to observe infants. Another of his well-known child portraits of his daughter, Maud (in the Museum of London), is also notable for its realism.

9 QUEEN VICTORIA

This lovely poured wax model of Queen Victoria as a young woman in coronation robes was purchased at the Great Exhibition of 1851. As it has always been kept under a glass dome, it is in excellent condition. The legs are made of cloth, with solid, possibly wooden, feet clad in bootees.

Underneath her well-fitted and trimmed silk dress, she wears a petticoat and pantalettes of pleated lawn and kid shoes. Her hair is real hair, inserted and braided in the fashion of the time. Her eyes are painted blue and there is a great deal of detail in the dress.

DATE	*c1851*
NATIONALITY	*English*
AVAILABILITY	*rare, expensive*
HEIGHT	*15in (38cm)*

This model resembles another model of Queen Victoria in the Museum of London, known to be by Madame Montanari, and this one could also be by this famous doll-maker. She was famous for the excellence of her costumes, and this elaborate gown with its lace and bead trimming is certainly the work of an experienced dressmaker. It would have been very expensive.

10 PRINCE OF WALES AND PRINCESS ROYAL

There was a tremendous interest in the royal family in the 19th century, and these two little dolls representing the older children were probably sold as souvenirs. They have solid wax heads and limbs and were made in Germany.

The Prince of Wales is wearing a white organza dress, as was the custom for baby boys of the time, with a hat of lace and gold decorated with princely feathers. His sister, the Princess Royal, wears a lace dress over blue satin and a plaited straw bonnet. Both wear lace pantalettes.

DATE	*c1843*
NATIONALITY	*German*
AVAILABILITY	*rare, expensive*
HEIGHT	*6in and 6½in (15cm and 16cm)*

Charming though they are, no attempt has been made to create portraits of the children; apart from their fine dress, they could be anybody.

11 LORD ROBERTS

Wax portrait dolls of famous people were as popular with the Victorians as were figures of the royal family. Lord Roberts was Commander-in-Chief of the British army during the Boer War, and Charles Pierotti made this lifelike model of him in 1901.

It is a convincing portrait of a military man at the height of his career, covered in medals, orders and gold braid as befits his rank. He has a wax head, arms and legs and his rather sparse hair and luxuriant moustache are inset. Charles Pierotti also made a wax model of King Edward VII in uniform at the time of his coronation, now in the Museum of London.

DATE
1901
NATIONALITY
English
AVAILABILITY
rare, expensive
HEIGHT
19in (48cm)

12 PRINCESS LOUISE AS A CHILD

In 1963 Vivien Greene bought a trunkful of clothes, letters, toys, books and other items from the daughter of the head nurse at Marlborough House, once the home of Alexandra, Princess of Wales. Among the fascinating ephemera it contained was this wax portrait doll of Princess Louise, Queen Victoria's granddaughter, as a child.

The doll is pale, with wax head and limbs and calico body. Underneath her white dress with its tucked bodice, she wears a cotton shift, lace-edged drawers, a cream flannel petticoat and a cambric half-petticoat with tucks and lace edging. On her feet she has silk shoes and socks and on her head, a cream silk bonnet. The maker is not known; it could have been by any of the prominent makers of wax dolls in London, though the slightly sulky expression suggests Meech.

There is an earlier portrait of Princess Louise aged about one year, in the Bethnal Green Museum of Childhood.

DATE
1870s
NATIONALITY
English
AVAILABILITY
rare, expensive
HEIGHT
22in (56cm)

12

PRINCESS LOUISA VICTORIA OF WALES.

13

14 WAX-HEADED DOLL

This beautiful doll has a wax head, bust and hands, while the rest of her body is of cloth stuffed with straw. The maker is unknown.

She has fixed brown eyes and arched eyebrows of individual hairs marked by indentation, giving her a sophisticated air. (In fact, she is much more sophisticated altogether than most other 18th-century dolls.) Her thick brown hair is topped by a cap of white muslin decorated with pink ribbons.

She wears a fashionable robe of pale turquoise silk, trimmed on the skirt with ribbons of the same silk. Her elbow-length sleeves have double cuffs of pinked ribbon and her V-neck bodice has detachable white muslin ruffles. The dress is worn over a taffeta waist petticoat quilted over cream wool and stays of thick white cotton stiffened with whalebone, a knee-length linen chemise with full-length sleeves, knitted knee-length wool stockings and red and gold needlepoint shoes with leather soles.

DATE
18th century
NATIONALITY
probably English
AVAILABILITY
rare, expensive
HEIGHT
24in (61cm)

13 LILLIE LANGTRY

This delightful poured wax portrait of Lillie Langtry, the famous Edwardian actress and mistress of Edward VII, is by an unknown maker. It was given to the owner of the Lilliput Museum by a woman who had worked for the famous actress and who had been given the doll as a memento of her late mistress.

The doll certainly does justice to the beauty of the "Jersey Lily", daughter of the Dean of Jersey, with her bright blue eyes and flawless complexion. It has to be said, however, that it must be an idealized portrait, for it does not resemble the painting of Lillie by Sir John Millais in the Jersey Museum. Her dress here appears to be late Edwardian, though she was the king's mistress in the 1870s and an actress in the 1880s, and she died in 1929.

The doll is dressed very plainly in outdoor clothing of a velvet cloak with fur trimming and beneath it is a white dress decorated with lace. Her hat is decorated with the remains of an ostrich feather.

DATE
c1900
NATIONALITY
English
AVAILABILITY
easy to find, mid-price range
HEIGHT
18in (46cm)

15 GILLIE CHARLSON BOY

Edward is one of a pair of twins which the well-known doll-maker, Gillie Charlson, copied from a Victorian photograph. Edward is wax throughout and has fixed glass eyes.

This artist works with her husband at her home near Chorley, Lancashire, where, as well as making dolls, she has a shop and holds seminars for aspiring doll-makers.

She often makes portraits of people, usually in a limited edition of 50, working sometimes in wax, sometimes in porcelain.

16 GLOVER MODERN DOLL

Girl with watering can by Margaret Glover, a well-known doll artist who lives in London, is based on a picture by the impressionist painter, Renoir, and both the painting and the doll are now in the USA.

The doll is made in the traditional poured wax manner, with inserted hair and eyelashes. Her dress is of velvet with antique lace and antique buttons, and she has handmade leather boots, also made by the artist.

In fact, Margaret Glover does everything herself – making the original, casting the wax, inserting the hair and dressing the dolls. She was unable to buy a miniature watering can, so created one for this doll out of an empty tube of soldering flux.

DATE
1970s
NATIONALITY
English
AVAILABILITY
*easy to find,
mid-price range*
HEIGHT
18in (46cm)

17 MODERN QUEEN VICTORIA

It is interesting to compare this wax version of the young Queen Victoria with the one on page 32.

The artist, Margaret Glover, had already dressed a Lucy Peck version of the young Queen for the late Betty Cadbury and had added a body and legs to a wax head of the Queen owned by another collector and dressed it, after which she decided to make this small version for herself, based on a contemporary print of the Queen.

This very fine and delicate doll, full of accurate detail in the coronation robes, is still in the possession of the artist.

DATE
1970s
NATIONALITY
English
AVAILABILITY
easy to find, inexpensive
HEIGHT
12in (30cm)

18 MARSHALL AND SNELGROVE DOLL

A pretty doll, known by the previous owner as the "Marshall and Snelgrove" doll, since she arrived in her original box with the name of that famous London store on it and the words "Child model wax doll". She also had her original clothing with her, a lawn dress with tucks and a lace top, a chemise, three petticoats and split-crutched drawers. Her head and shoulders are made of poured wax, and she has composition arms and legs and a soft body stuffed with hair. Her mohair curls were inserted into her head and she has fixed blue glass eyes and an open mouth with teeth.

DATE
1870
NATIONALITY
German
AVAILABILITY
rare, expensive
HEIGHT
24in (61cm)

She was made by Cuno & Otto Dressel of Sonneberg, Germany, and bears their Holz-Masse mark on her thigh. She cost £1 ($1.70) at that time.

19 FASHION DOLLS

 These two solid wax dolls were probably made for Harrods department store in London in the 1920s. They were made solely for advertising clothes, so they do not move at all, but the one on the left is dressed elegantly, and has her coat carelessly hung over the back of the chair.

The doll on the right is dressed in pierrot costume, in the style of a boudoir doll.

DATE
c1924
NATIONALITY
English
AVAILABILITY
rare, inexpensive
HEIGHT
approx 14in (35.5cm)

19

20 CRÈCHE FIGURE

20

 Crèche figures were made by artists for religious purposes, but as they are almost the only dolls to survive from early years, they are of great interest to doll collectors.

Crèche groups were made all over Europe, out of various materials including wood, terracotta and wax. Some were very large and ornate, composed of dozens of figures dressed in rich clothing; others were quite small, made for private houses.

This figure has a wax head and carved wooden hands. She is wearing a brocade dress decorated with silver lace, so was clearly a person of importance in the group, possibly the wife of the person who had commissioned it.

DATE
c1780
NATIONALITY
German
AVAILABILITY
rare, expensive
HEIGHT
12in (30cm)

21 SOLID WAX DOLL

This tiny doll, made of solid wax and sitting in its high chair holding a flower in its hand, is one of the oldest dolls in the Museum Simon van Gijn, Dordrecht, the Netherlands. It could date from the early 18th century.

One can only guess at the purpose of this little figure, which might have been a portrait of some child, or simply intended as an ornament. It seems safe to say that it was never played with as a toy, since it is in such excellent condition, though it might have survived by being tucked out of sight at the back of a doll's house room.

DATE
c1800
NATIONALITY
Dutch
AVAILABILITY
rare, expensive
HEIGHT
(doll) 2¼in (5.5cm)

23 GERMAN WAX DOLL

A pretty German doll dating from about 1880, wearing her original clothing and with her original hair. (You can see insertions around the forehead.) The eyes are fixed; the mouth is open to reveal teeth. The doll is wearing a pale blue dress with a white insert, decorated with pearl beads. A bead crucifix hangs from her pearl necklace.

DATE
c1880
NATIONALITY
German
AVAILABILITY
*easy to find,
mid-price range*
HEIGHT
approx 18in (46cm)

22 CHARLES MARSH DOLL

A Charles Marsh doll, dating from about 1880 and dressed as a bride. The head and hands are of wax but the generously proportioned body is made of cloth. The hair and eyebrows are inserted in the traditional way and the fixed glass eyes are blue. It is stamped with the Charles Marsh stamp and the Royal Warrant.

Brides were a popular subject for wax doll-makers, probably because they presented such an opportunity for pretty dresses with plenty of frills and furbelows. It is thought that the clothing on earlier Marsh dolls was made by members of the Marsh family, though little seems to be known about them, or, indeed, about Charles Marsh.

DATE
c1880
NATIONALITY
English
AVAILABILITY
rare, expensive
HEIGHT
19in (48cm)

24 WAX WITH GLASS EYES

 One of the 1,200 dolls in the collection at the Judges' Lodgings, in Lancaster. The Museum of Childhood is on the second floor of the 17th-century building, which was once used to accommodate visiting circuit judges attending the nearby assizes.

This charming little wax doll has fixed glass eyes and brown curly hair. She is wearing a light summer dress of white cotton and a large straw sunbonnet tied beneath the chin with a ribbon bow.

DATE
1820
NATIONALITY
English
AVAILABILITY
rare, expensive
HEIGHT
12in (30cm)

25 PRINCESS CAROLINE

 A wax-over-composition doll wearing a dress made by a lady-in-waiting to Princess Caroline of Brunswick, wife of the Prince Regent of England, who became George IV in 1820. For a short time, Princess Caroline was Queen of England, though she was not allowed into Westminster Abbey for the coronation. Theirs was an unhappy marriage.

The material from which the doll's dress is made was a remnant of this unfortunate lady's wedding dress, a pretty cream, green and silver brocade decorated with lace. It was fashioned to resemble the Princess's dress. She is what is known as a slit-head, that is, a slit was cut in the head of this type of wax-over-composition doll and the hair was inserted into it to fall down on either side of the face. She has fixed blue glass eyes, a cloth body and wax arms and is in remarkably good condition for her age.

DATE
c1790
NATIONALITY
English
AVAILABILITY
rare, expensive
HEIGHT
26in (66cm)

26 SLIT-HEAD DOLL

 One of the characteristics of slit-head wax-over-composition dolls is their happy expression, and this doll, with her chubby face and fixed blue glass eyes, is no exception.

She is wearing a lace-trimmed white dress and a straw bonnet. Underneath her dress she wears a full set of underwear. She arrived complete with a trousseau of seven sets of clothes.

DATE
c1840
NATIONALITY
English
AVAILABILITY
easy to find, mid-price range
HEIGHT
approx 26in (66cm)

27 TWO-FACED DOLL

Fritz Bartenstein of Germany specialized in two- and three-faced dolls in different materials. A pull-string through the cylindrical body turns the head round to reveal a crying or a smiling face beneath the fixed hood, which is covered by a bonnet.

This doll has a cloth body, but there were different varieties, such as cloth-over-composition, cardboard or wax-over-papier mâché. It is wearing a long baby robe decorated with tucks and lace and a cloak with a hood that covers the moving mechanism.

DATE
1880
NATIONALITY
German
AVAILABILITY
rare, expensive
HEIGHT
14in (35.5cm)

27

28 QUEEN VICTORIA'S DAUGHTER'S DOLL

A beautifully dressed wax-over-papier-mâché doll said to have belonged to Queen Victoria's eldest daughter, Vicky. She has sleeping eyes, which are worked by a wire hidden in one of her wrists.

As well as being exquisitely attired in her striped silk dress, the doll has been well modelled, with toe and finger nails clearly defined on her wax feet and hands. Her hair is real hair, arranged in ringlets which fall from a stitched base on the head.

DATE
c1845
NATIONALITY
English
AVAILABILITY
easy to find, mid-price range
HEIGHT
19in (48cm)

29 PUMPKIN HEAD AND BONNET

DATE
c1850
NATIONALITY
German
AVAILABILITY
easy to find mid-price range
HEIGHT
large, 18in (46cm); small, 12in (30.5cm)

These two wax-over-composition dolls are typical of their kind. The taller doll is what is known as a pumpkin head, because of the broad face and a head that is flat from back to front, since it was made in a shallow mould.

This doll is wearing a hair band on her moulded blonde hair and has carved wooden hands and forearms and carved wooden lower legs ending in flat-heeled boots with painted buttons. She has the dark pupil-less eyes popular in the 1860s and is dressed in a flannel pin-tucked dress over three petticoats and split-crutch drawers.

The smaller doll is a bonnet wax-over-composition doll, with a Motschmann-type body. A bonnet doll is one with hat and hair moulded in one. The hat is decorated with three feathers and a snood.

The small doll has wooden forearms and wooden lower legs ending in painted flat-heeled boots. She has on her original lawn cotton dress with two petticoats beneath. Her glass eyes are brown.

30 PEDLAR DOLL

This little wax-over-composition pedlar doll has been kept under a glass dome to protect her and her wares from dust.

In one of her hands she is holding a pack of playing cards, while her basket is filled with an assortment of useful items such as knitting wool, ribbons, writing paper, buttons and shoe laces, as well as things to please the children like a small peg doll and a porcelain Frozen Charlotte doll.

DATE
c1848
NATIONALITY
English
AVAILABILITY
*easy to find,
mid-price range*
HEIGHT
approx 12in (30cm)

31 MRS HERBERT'S DOLLS

This amusing group of wax-over-composition dolls was dressed by the ladies of the Sultan of Baghdad's harem in 1868. They were presented to the harem, in an unclothed state, by Mrs Herbert, the British Resident's wife, who was horrified to learn that the ladies had no occupation at all, apart from quarrelling among themselves, and sent to London for some dolls for them to dress. General and Mrs Herbert eventually retired to Tunbridge Wells, England.

The doll on the left, wearing black silk trousers, is a German Motschmann talking doll, with bellows concealed in the waist and a squeaking mechanism. Another German talking doll is wearing a striped silk robe, patterned sash and a red turban. The doll in the lavender-coloured dress is English, and the doll wearing the long striped coat, with gold around its neck, is German.

DATE
c1868
NATIONALITY
German and English
AVAILABILITY
*easy to find,
mid-price range*
HEIGHT
*16–26in
(40.5–66cm)*

32 BRIDE AND BRIDESMAID

This happy pair of slit-heads represents a bride and her bridesmaid. They were owned by the donor's husband's great-grandmother and are now in the Lilliput Museum, Isle of Wight, UK.

They have wax-over-composition heads and cloth bodies with coloured leather arms. Wires protruding from the dolls' chests can be pulled to open and close their eyes.

They are wearing their original clothing and, apart from a little crazing, are in remarkably good condition.

DATE
c1840–50
NATIONALITY
English
AVAILABILITY
*easy to find
mid-price range*
HEIGHT
28in (71cm)

33

33 STRAW-DRESSED DOLLS

 A most unusual doll, with a wax-over-composition head, black glass eyes and very basic composition arms. It seems unlikely that there could be a body underneath the elaborate costume, which dates to about 1880. She is surrounded by straw flowers and is wearing an elegant outfit of a plaited straw cape and dress and a straw hat. This and several other similar dolls are to be seen in the Wardown Park Museum, Luton, England. The town was a centre of the straw hat-making industry in the 18th and 19th centuries. The origin of the dolls is something of a mystery, as is their nationality, since there are no identifying marks on them, but they may have been made for one of the many local exhibitions of straw work held to encourage the plaiting industry towards the end of the 19th century.

DATE
c1880
NATIONALITY
not known
AVAILABILITY
rare, expensive
HEIGHT
9in (23cm)

34 WAX-OVER-PAPIER MÂCHÉ DOLL

 A handsome wax-over-papier mâché doll wearing a white cotton dress decorated with a tartan trim and pompons. Her face is finely modelled and painted, and her brown hair is set in wax. She has brown glass eyes and nice pink cheeks.

In this picture you can see clearly where the shoulder-plate ends and joins the cloth body to which the wooden arms are attached.

Wax was expensive in the 19th century and dipping a papier mâché doll head in wax to give it a fine finish was an efficient form of economy.

DATE
1850–55
NATIONALITY
German
AVAILABILITY
easy to find, mid-price range
HEIGHT
15in (38cm)

34

35

35 WAX AND WAX-OVER DOLLS

 The doll in the blue striped dress and straw hat tied under the chin with ribbon is made of poured wax, with the curiously long upper arms typical of so many wax dolls of the late 19th century. She is holding a parasol which matches her dress. In her rear pocket is a hemmed handkerchief and she has a full set of underwear and leather shoes.

The doll in the white dress is made of wax-over-composition and she has composition arms and legs and fixed eyes. The dress is an elaborate one, trimmed with white satin ribbons and lace; underneath she is wearing a full set of underclothes including three petticoats and lace-edged drawers. Both dolls date from about 1880.

DATE
c1880
NATIONALITY
English
AVAILABILITY
rare, expensive, and easy to find, mid-price range
HEIGHT
8in (20cm)

36 SLIT-HEAD DOLL

 Another slit-head wax-over-papier mâché doll with ringlets falling from the centre parting. Here you can see a slight crazing on the forehead, which was caused by the expansion and contraction of the papier mâché beneath the wax.

A great many of these dolls were produced in the early 19th century. As only the head and shoulder-plates were dipped in wax and the bodies were made of fabric, with the arms often encased in leather gloves up to the elbow, they were cheap to make. The more expensive versions would have had wax-over-composition limbs.

Most of these attractive dolls have fixed, dark, pupil-less eyes and a smiling mouth.

> DATE
> *mid-19th century*
> NATIONALITY
> *English*
> AVAILABILITY
> *easy to find, mid-price range*
> HEIGHT
> *19in (47.5cm)*

37 WAX-OVER-PAPIER MÂCHÉ DOLL

 Wearing her original dress, this large wax-over-papier mâché doll is of better quality than the one on page 42. She has well-shaped wax-over-papier mâché arms and legs which end in a pair of neat little red boots.

Her fixed blue eyes have pupils and her mouth is unsmiling, all of which indicate that she is a later doll.

> DATE
> *c1870*
> NATIONALITY
> *probably French*
> AVAILABILITY
> *easy to find, mid-price range*
> HEIGHT
> *29in (72.5cm)*

36

37

38 BONNET HEAD

 A perfect example of a bonnet head wax-over-papier mâché doll. The hat, decorated with a feather, is moulded in with the head.

Dolls can be found wearing many varieties of hat; some with three feathers, some tricorn-shaped and some shaped like a top hat, again with a large feather on the crown. There are also boy bonnet dolls.

> DATE
> *1840–60s*
> NATIONALITY
> *probably German*
> AVAILABILITY
> *easy to find, mid-price range*
> HEIGHT
> *15in (38cm)*

39 BARTENSTEIN DOLL

Although he is famous for his two-faced dolls, Fritz Bartenstein also made other, less innovative wax dolls. This wax-over-papier mâché doll is probably one of them.

The doll has well-defined fingers and a pleasing face with an open mouth showing two teeth.

DATE
c1880
NATIONALITY
German
AVAILABILITY
easy to find, mid-price range
HEIGHT
20in (51cm)

39

40 BRIDE

A wax-over-papier mâché bride with a straw-filled body and short composition arms and composition legs.

Her mohair wig is glued to a carton pate and her glass eyes are fixed. Her bridal gown, underwear, shoes and socks are all original. The dress is made of oyster paper taffeta with lace trimming. She is wearing a head-dress and carrying a bouquet of small wax flowers.

DATE
c1880
NATIONALITY
probably English
AVAILABILITY
easy to find, mid-price range
HEIGHT
23in (58.5cm)

40

41 MAZAWATTEE TEA DOLL

Advertising gimmicks were well under way by the middle of the 19th century and this pumpkin-headed wax-over-composition doll was given away as a free gift with packets of tea in the 1860s.

She has wooden spade hands, arms and legs and a cloth body.

DATE
1860s
NATIONALITY
English
AVAILABILITY
easy to find, mid-price range
HEIGHT
16in (41cm)

41

Papier Mâché and Composition

Papier mâché (literally, chewed paper) is a paper pulp substance mixed with water, resulting in a lightweight, inexpensive mixture which can be pressed into moulds. Some form of filler is usually added, such as flour, meal, sand, clay, whiting or chalk, and the whole mixture is bound together with glue or starch paste.

Since paper is attractive to insects and rodents, the manufacturers tried to make it less so by adding oils and repellents and varnishing or waxing the dolls. Both of these methods were successful in the short term, though papier mâché dolls have not lasted well over the years and those dipped in wax have developed cracks. Damp and excessive heat are also both enemies of this substance.

Papier mâché was used as a material for making votive figures in Italy in the 15th and 16th centuries. In his book *Dolls* (written in 1929), Max von Boehn mentioned a collection of such figures in the church of S. Maria delle Grazie in Mantua, Italy. Papier mâché was used for crèche figures in the early 18th century and for dolls a little later. In England factories were making small decorative items made of paper pulp in the 1700s.

Between 1810 and 1852, F.G. Volkmar of Ilmenau, Germay, made many of the early types of papier mâché doll heads with hair arranged in elaborate swirls and buns moulded into the head and painted black.

Heads like these, known to collectors as milliners' models for no very good reason, are found on a variety of bodies, on calico bodies with kid arms and on all-kid bodies with wooden lower limbs. The heads continued to be made until the 1840s and dolls with these heads are a desirable addition to a collection.

Mid-19th century German dolls are quite different in style from and are not nearly as pretty as the earlier ones. They are child dolls with plump faces and thick necks, often with bamboo teeth and not much in the way of hair. Their bodies are made of leather and are probably French. They are filled with sawdust or straw. Charles Motschmann, famous for his dolls with limbs and bodies jointed with cloth, also made heads of papier mâché to go on his unusual bodies, though he progressed to heads of wood and porcelain.

Papier mâché ceased to be a popular material for dolls in Europe after the middle of the 19th century but it did enjoy a revival in America. A German doll-maker named Ludwig Greiner set himself up in business in Philadelphia, where the raw materials of his trade were readily obtainable. His first patent for a papier mâché doll's head was issued in 1858, though it is thought that he and his family had been producing dolls for some time before that date. Early Greiner heads are made of paper, whiting and flour, mixed with glue and reinforced with linen. They have moulded, wavy black hair with a centre parting, painted or glass eyes and rather matronly faces. Their finish was very durable, so Greiner dolls are often found in good condition, primarily in the USA, and rarely in Europe, as they were not exported.

Composition

Composition is a word used to describe a modelling material made of various substances, and over the years many different types have been used to make dolls. Among the materials used to make composition were plaster of Paris, bran and sawdust bound together with glue. In 1887 a German manufacturer in Sonneberg applied for a patent to make doll's heads out of a paste board known as leather board, which was to be placed in hot press moulds and submitted to high pressure.

Composition was also used as a base for wax heads, which were dipped in the wax as a means of making them more attractive yet less expensive than poured wax.

Early composition dolls had limbs made of the same material as the head, fitted to a cloth body, in the same way that shoulder-headed bisques were made. Later, the manufacturers added all-composition bodies.

In the early years of the 20th century, wood composition became the widely accepted material for doll-making and there are many examples of this type of doll in Europe and in America. Wood composition was cheap to produce, could be given a good finish and was quite strong, but on the other hand it absorbed moisture, causing the covering paint to crack.

Several modern doll-artists have experimented with papier mâché and composition. One interesting French craftswoman was Berthe Noufflard, who worked during the early part of the 20th century. Her dolls, which have heads made of a kind of thick plaster, were made in very limited numbers because she was not able to interest any doll manufacturer in them or to manufacture them herself on a large scale. However, some of these unusual dolls have survived and are in the Musée des Arts Décoratifs in Paris.

There is a long tradition of doll-making in Japan. Most of the dolls belong to the category of Hina dolls used for the Girls' Doll Festival in March, but there are also the dolls which developed as toys such as the Mitsuore doll, with jointed hips, legs and arms, and the Yamoto doll, many of which were sent to children of the United States from the children of Japan as envoys of goodwill over 60 years ago.

Caring for papier mâché and composition dolls

In her book *Understanding Dolls* Caroline Goodfellow points out that the main disadvantage of composition is that it is difficult to clean. The top coat of varnish, which most such dolls were given, can be adversely affected by water. She advises rubbing soft white bread gently over the surface, which will remove the grime without injuring the doll, "Should you attempt to try to clean it yourself, please remember not to scrub."

It is also possible to use a liquid cleaning product, whipped into a foam and using the foam only. If you do this, test a small, inconspicuous area with the cleaner before you begin, particularly before you touch the face. Apply the foam to a clean, soft white cloth, not to the surface of the doll. Check the cloth frequently to ensure that no colour is "lifting". Use a different section of the cloth each time you apply it. Do not soak the doll. Rinse off the foam with a cloth slightly moistened in distilled water. Always work very slowly and carefully.

Papier mâché and composition dolls should be examined for signs of infestation by insects from time to time and the use of an insecticide in storage is advisable. There are many excellent products available. Store the dolls in a dry place in an even temperature. If you wrap them, use an acid-free tissue paper.

The faces of papier mâché and composition dolls are often found with chipped noses and rubbed areas. Unfortunately, there is not much to be done about this, since any repair stands little chance of matching up with the original surface. However, some doll owners who are dextrous with their hands have successfully used plastic wood to repair chips.

Collecting papier mâché and composition dolls

Early papier mâché dolls are not by any means cheap, nor are they plentiful. Greiners are not easily obtainable in Europe; they are more often found in the USA.

Later composition dolls are a better hunting area for collectors. Ten years ago few collectors would have considered adding a 1920s or 1930s composition doll to a collection, yet as recently as 1992 an Ideal composition Shirley Temple doll was sold at auction in the USA for $1400 (£823). At the same time, a box which had contained a Shirley Temple doll was sold for $100 (£69), which is a lesson to collectors to keep the packaging of all their dolls, old or new.

1 EARLY PAPIER-MÂCHÉ DOLL WITH WATCH

 The elegant striped silk dress of this papier mâché doll helps to date her to the second half of the 18th century. The original dress is of the open robe type, with a second skirt under the first.

Beneath the dress she is wearing two linen petticoats, silk stockings and black silk shoes with buckles. Her face is painted and her body and arms are made of leather. Other details are her beads, bead earrings and bead rings and a watch dangling from her waist. She is clearly a lady of some consequence.

DATE
c1780
NATIONALITY
English
AVAILABILITY
rare, expensive
HEIGHT
18½in (47cm)

2 BLACK-HAIRED DOLL

 A Regency papier mâché doll with black moulded hair dressed in an elaborate style. She has a leather body and wooden arms and is wearing her original dress, which is decorated with a pattern of feathers and trimmed with lace at the neck, sleeves and hem.

The cost of making a papier mâché doll would have been higher than making a wooden doll, because of factory overheads. Papier mâché dolls with this hairstyle are sometimes known as Queen Adelaide dolls, after the wife of William IV. Drawings and paintings of the time show that women did actually wear their hair in this style.

DATE
c1810
NATIONALITY
English
AVAILABILITY
rare, expensive
HEIGHT
10½in (27cm)

3 SPIJK MIJNSSEN DOLL

 A doll with a papier mâché head, wooden arms and cloth body, which was made by Spijk Mijnssen in 1800.

She is wearing a tucked pink tunic dress over a white blouse. Her face is very pale, with just a touch of colour in the lips.

DATE
1800
NATIONALITY
Dutch
AVAILABILITY
rare, expensive
HEIGHT
21¾in (55cm)

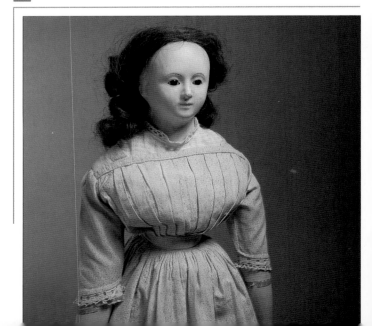

5

4 GENERAL VALLÉE DOLL

This elegant papier mâché doll belonged to the wife of the first French governor of Algeria, General Valée, in 1837.

She has a papier mâché head, leather body and dark, fixed glass eyes. She is wearing a cotton mousseline dress with leg-of-mutton sleeves, which would have been typical of the light tropical clothing worn by European women in Algeria at that time.

DATE
1837
NATIONALITY
French
AVAILABILITY
rare, expensive
HEIGHT
19¼in (48.5cm)

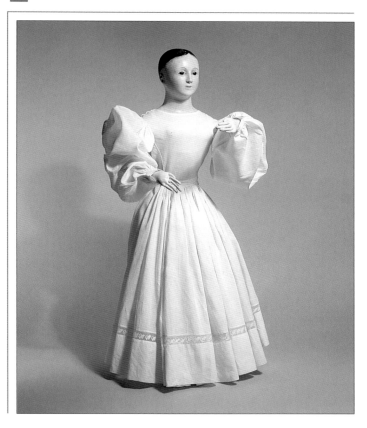

5 HORSMAN CAN'T BREAK 'EM FAIRY DOLL

A Fairy doll designed by Helen Trowbridge and produced by Horsman from 1911. It represents the figure advertised by N. K. Fairbanks Co. for its Little Fairy Soap. It has a composition head and hands on a cloth body, moulded bobbed hair with a curl on its forehead and painted features. The hands are the early Campbell Kid type.

The Can't Break 'Em composition dolls by Horsman were described as "with heads modelled from life by an American sculptress and such original models duly protected by copyright". The composition from which the dolls were made was a closely guarded secret.

DATE
c1911
NATIONALITY
American
AVAILABILITY
easy to find, mid-price range
HEIGHT
13in (33cm)

6 WELL-DRESSED DOLL

This sumptuously dressed papier mâché doll of fine quality from the early 19th century must surely have been dressed by a professional needlewoman. The bodice is heavily beaded and the elaborate hat, in the fashion of the 1820s, is decorated with ribbons and lace.

The hair is moulded and the face delicately painted, with painted eyes, and the arms are wooden.

The dressed doll could have been a dressmaker's sample, which was sent, perhaps, to some rich lady to demonstrate the maker's sewing skills.

DATE
c1825
NATIONALITY
English
AVAILABILITY
rare, expensive
HEIGHT
13in (33cm)

7 DARK-HAIRED DOLL

The face of this papier-mâché-headed doll with glazed porcelain arms is similar to that of the doll on page 49. It, too has moulded black hair and dark, fixed, glass eyes.

It is dressed in a child's dress of white cotton printed with red spots, and is wearing pantalettes and a petticoat decorated with lace.

DATE
1825–50
NATIONALITY
probably German
AVAILABILITY
easy to find
mid-price range
HEIGHT
15in (38cm)

8 PAPIER MÂCHÉ DOLL

Looking elegant in her white linen dress with lace trimming, this doll with a papier mâché head has upper arms and legs of kid leather. The lower arms are made of wood. Her hair, fashioned severely with a bun at the back, is moulded with the head and she has bright blue eyes and tinted cheeks.

Many dolls of this type are damaged, as they crack easily.

DATE
1840–45
NATIONALITY
English
AVAILABILITY
easy to find,
mid-price range
HEIGHT
10½in (27cm)

9 PULL-STRING DOLL

A walking, talking, kiss-blowing doll, with a pull-string mechanisms. She has a composition head and body, glass eyes and her own original wig. Her underclothing is scant and would always have been so, as the child had to be able to get at the string to pull it. The string works from the hip and the doll walks along, calling "Mama" and "Papa" while blowing kisses.

She is unmarked but closely resembles the SFBJ character dolls and is probably a member of the same family.

DATE
c1905
NATIONALITY
French
AVAILABILITY
easy to find,
mid-price range
HEIGHT
20in (51cm)

10

11 GREINER DOLL II

Early papier mâché-headed Greiners usually have black hair parted down the middle, like the German porcelain dolls of the period, but later there were variations on the hairstyles.

The dolls have slightly chubby, rather matronly faces like this one. Some of the heads had glass eyes but these are painted blue. The doll has a cloth body, leather arms and a patent label "58" on the back of her shoulders. She is wearing a dress made from old fabric. Greiner varnished his dolls, which means that they have lasted better than many others of this material. The Greiner family was involved in the doll-making business until 1900.

DATE
c1850
NATIONALITY
American
AVAILABILITY
easy to find mid-price range
HEIGHT
11½in (29cm)

12

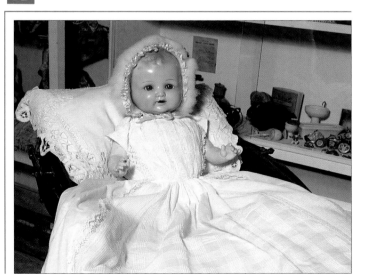

10 GREINER DOLL

Ludwig Greiner was a German by birth, who emigrated to the USA where he started a factory to make dolls' heads out of papier mâché. The bodies were often left for others to make, so there is a wide variety of them, some homemade and others made by local commercial firms.

This doll has moulded hair, painted eyes, leather arms and stuffed legs, and she is quite large.

Greiner made dolls for sale in the USA and did not export to Europe. His first patent was dated 1858, but it is thought that he was making doll's heads for some time before that date.

DATE
c1845
NATIONALITY
American
AVAILABILITY
easy to find, mid-price range
HEIGHT
24in (61cm)

11

12 ARMAND MARSEILLE DOLL

Armand Marseille died in 1925 but his firm continued to produce dolls for many years under the direction of his son, Hermann, making composition heads as well as bisque.

This Armand Marseille bent-limbed composition baby doll was once offered as a gift for one of her children to Queen Victoria, who ungraciously refused it. It has an open mouth and dark blue sleeping eyes and it is dressed in a white tucked christening robe and a fur-trimmed bonnet.

DATE
c1880
NATIONALITY
German
AVAILABILITY
easy to find, mid-price range
HEIGHT
approx 16in (40cm)

13 COMPOSITION BOY DOLL

A composition boy doll dressed in his original clothes, dating from about 1940. He has moulded curly hair, short stubby fingers and toes, painted eyes, bent limbs and an open-closed mouth. His original blue checked shirt and brown short trousers have been made by a professional. He also possesses a cap and a buttoned jacket to match his trousers. He is typical of the kind of doll being made in the UK at this time.

DATE
1940s
NATIONALITY
English
AVAILABILITY
easy to find, inexpensive
HEIGHT
15in (38cm)

14 BOUDOIR DOLL

Boudoir or Art dolls made in this century were intended as adult toys and were used to decorate fashionable ladies' bedrooms.
This one has a composition head and hands and a cloth body, which dould be made to sit in any position. It also has knitted silk stockings and bronze leather shoes and is holding a mandolin that plays music when wound up.
Some boudoir dolls had painted cloth faces, some are dressed in exotic fashions, others in the styles of the 1920s.

DATE
1920s
NATIONALITY
probably French
AVAILABILITY
rare, inexpensive
HEIGHT
25½in (65cm)

15

15 SHIRLEY TEMPLE

There must have been hundreds of different doll versions of the child film star of the 1930s, Shirley Temple. This version does not resemble her as closely as some, and the characteristic Shirley curls seem to have suffered from fall-out over the years. However, she is marked "13 Shirley Temple" and she was made by the Ideal Toy Corp., New York. Ideal introduced the doll in 1934 and by the following year mothers all over the world were trying to make their daughters into clones of Shirley Temples, not always with success since those curls were difficult to achieve. Ideal reissued the doll in the 1950s in hard plastic and vinyl.

DATE
1934–39
NATIONALITY
American
AVAILABILITY
easy to find
inexpensive
HEIGHT
13in (33cm)

16 POST-WAR DOLLS

The large doll with the crazed face is a Pedigree composition bent-limb baby with sleeping eyes and the other two are pot heads with bent-limb bodies – the one on the left has cloth limbs and you can see the line of the mould in which he was cast running down the side of the head.

Pedigree was the first firm in England to manufacture high quality composition dolls by factory methods, advertising them as "almost unbreakable". They all have arms and legs jointed at hips and shoulders.

DATE
1950s
NATIONALITY
English
AVAILABILITY
rare, inexpensive
HEIGHT
12–17in (30–43cm)

16

17 DIONNE QUINS

DATE
1934
NATIONALITY
American
AVAILABILITY
easy to find,
mid-price range
HEIGHT
7½in (19cm)

Just as famous as Miss Temple in their day were the Dionne Quins, who were born in 1934 in Callender, Ontario, Canada. Their names were Annette, Cecile, Emelie, Marie and Yvonne and the Madame Alexander Doll Company secured sole rights to make doll models of them, though some other versions were made in Japan and Germany.

This set of composition quins shows them as babies, with bent limbs, painted brown eyes glancing sideways and moulded hair. They are wearing their original clothing, including bibs with their names embroidered on them. The five nightgowns and the bed were part of the set.

At least one other size was made of the quins, who were very pretty little toddlers as can be seen from the book about them in the photograph, which shows them at two-years-old. As babies have a tendency to look much alike, many a mother must have bought five identical baby dolls and dressed them, rather than pay for a commercially made set.

18 IDEAL SHIRLEY TEMPLE

This version of Shirley Temple is more attractive because of the curls, but the face is the same. The doll has green sleeping eyes and is marked "CDP Ideal". The teeth can clearly be seen in the smiling mouth. There must still be hundreds of these dolls in existence, for the Shirley Temple craze lasted right up to 1939, with a small revival following to the re-showing of her films in the 1950s. Other child film stars came and went, but no one ever came near her for popularity.

DATE
c1934
NATIONALITY
American
AVAILABILITY
*easy to find,
mid-price range*
HEIGHT
18in (46cm)

19 JAPANESE BOY

A Japanese boy doll with composition head and body, real, black, straight hair and fixed glass eyes. He is wearing his original well-made kimono, and has bent limbs and an open/closed mouth.

He has what is known as a gofun – covered face – that is, a finish which is resistant to changes in temperature and humidity, though the surface can crack and should therefore be treated carefully.

A growing number of Japanese antique dealers are now adding old dolls to their other items for sale.

DATE
c1930
NATIONALITY
Japanese
AVAILABILITY
*easy to find
inexpensive*
HEIGHT
7in (18cm)

18

19

 20 CZECHOSLOVAKIAN DOLL

A charming doll in Czechoslovakian national costume, which was given to the owner just after she was born in that country. She now lives in England as do her parents, who left Czechoslovakia when she was quite young.

The doll has a composition face and cloth body and limbs and, considering how difficult it was to obtain raw materials for anything just after World War II, she is very well made. The body, arms and legs are firmly stuffed and the finish is good. She has a real hair wig stuck on top of moulded hair. The costume is interesting. The doll is wearing a white puff-sleeved blouse with lace at the neck and arms, a ribbon belt and a red skirt decorated with three different types of braid. Underneath this are a linen petticoat and drawers, both decorated with fancy stitching. On her head is a crown of flowers from which ribbons hang.

DATE
1947
NATIONALITY
Czechoslovakian
AVAILABILITY
rare, inexpensive
HEIGHT
15in (38cm)

21

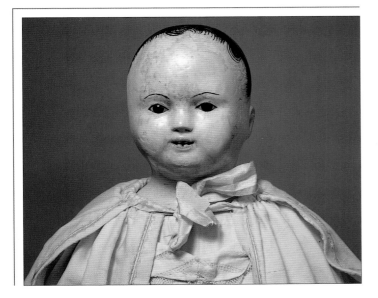

 21 DOLL WITH BAMBOO TEETH

A typical mid-19th century doll, probably with a German head on a French body. She has a well-made, gusseted leather body, glass eyes, painted hair and top and bottom bamboo teeth. (Gussets were added to enable the doll to sit convincingly.)

The doll is not particularly attractive, and the teeth do not add much to her appearance. Bamboo, glass, porcelain and wood were some of the materials commonly used for teeth on this type of doll.

DATE
c1850–60
NATIONALITY
German
AVAILABILITY
easy to find, mid-price range
HEIGHT
25in (63.5cm)

22

 MILLINER'S MODEL

Dolls like this, with elaborate hairstyles of various kinds, are often known as Milliner's models, though there does not seem to be any reason to think that they were. Many of them have leather bodies and wooden limbs and range in size from 16in to 20in (41cm to 51cm).

The hairstyles were fashionable up to about 1820, but the dolls would have continued to be manufactured after this date, regardless of fashion.

This one is wearing her original white dress with lace insets and a long drab-coloured cloak. The arms and legs are made of leather.

DATE
c1840–50
NATIONALITY
German
AVAILABILITY
easy to find, mid-price range
HEIGHT
20in (51cm)

23 IDEAL SNOW WHITE

 This Ideal Toy Corp., Snow White has a composition head and body, a hair ribbon moulded in with the hair, socket neck, green eyes with brown lashes, black brows, an open mouth showing four teeth and black mohair hair. She is wearing her original red dress with a cape, slip and panties, white socks, black shoes and a taffeta skirt printed with the logo "Snow White and the Seven Dwarfs, WD Enterprises". Ideal made another version of this doll, in all cloth, with a glued-on wig.

DATE
c1937
NATIONALITY
American
AVAILABILITY
*easy to find
mid-price range*
HEIGHT
13in (33cm)

24 EFFANBEE BUBBLES

 An Effanbee Bubbles all-composition doll, wearing its original dress and bonnet and a pair of knitted bootees. This series of dolls had cry voices, open mouths, two teeth showing, elongated bodies and well-defined dimples.

Effanbee dolls were made by the firm of Fleischaker & Baum from 1910, which produced a great variety of dolls, usually with the trademark on them, which is a help to collectors.

DATE
1925
NATIONALITY
American
AVAILABILITY
*easy to find,
inexpensive*
HEIGHT
14in (36cm)

25 POLISH SOLDIER

 A soldier doll in its original khaki-coloured uniform, which is probably Polish. It has a papier mâché shoulder-head on a soft cloth body, felt hands and stuffed cloth legs and arms. The features are painted. The doll is thought to have been made in England. During World War II a great many Polish soldiers served with the British forces, some settling in the country afterwards.

DATE
c1940
NATIONALITY
English
AVAILABILITY
rare, inexpensive
HEIGHT
19in (48cm)

26 THAILAND DOLLS

The former owner of these Thai dancing dolls travelled extensively and often brought home dolls depicting the customs and costumes of the different cultures she encountered.

Made of papier mâché, decorated with a rich profusion of gold braid, gold fabric and glittering sequins, the dolls are known as Monkey Dancers. They form a dramatic group when seen in an English setting.

DATE
20th century
NATIONALITY
Thai
AVAILABILITY
rare, expensive
HEIGHT
14in (36cm)

26

27 OLIVE WHITE DOLL

 A doll with a papier mâché head on a cloth body by Olive White, the widow of the author James Dillington White. She took up doll-making as a hobby to occupy her time while her husband was writing and evolved her own method of making dolls, using the simplest of materials which cost little.

Using an existing doll head, she placed layers of thin tissue paper on to the greased head, hardening it with wallpaper adhesive and white PVA adhesive. When using this technique, it is important not to add too many layers of papers, or the features will become blurred.

DATE
1983
NATIONALITY
English
AVAILABILITY
easy to find, mid-price range
HEIGHT
approx 14in (36cm)

28 BERTHE NOUFFLARD DOLL

 Berthe Noufflard (born 1886) was a painter who was particularly interested in portraiture. Her first dolls, made about 1915, were displayed in the Musée des Arts Décoratifs in Paris. They were made of composition and plaster, as were the articulated legs, arms and some of the bodies, which makes them heavy. The hair was mohair and the painted faces have a charming, child-like air.

Berthe Noufflard tried unsuccessfully to interest SFBJ in producing her dolls, and although she had planned to make a series of different types of doll, the heads that remain today seem to be from only three moulds.

DATE
c1916
NATIONALITY
French
AVAILABILITY
rare, expensive
HEIGHT
16½in (42cm)

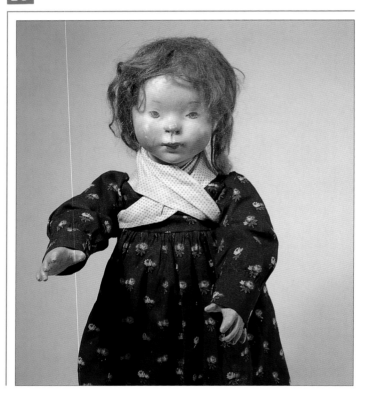

29 ROSI

 A charming composition doll dressed in her original 1930s clothes and wearing her original abundant wig. She is German and is jointed at the neck, shoulders, elbows, wrists and hips. Not very much is known about her, except that she has the name "Rosi" scratched on the back of her neck.

DATE
1930s
NATIONALITY
German
AVAILABILITY
easy to find, mid-price range
HEIGHT
17in (43cm)

30 ## ITALIAN DOLL

30

A rare 17th- or 18th-century doll made of moulded "carton" or composition, not wood, coated with gesso and painted. The dress is painted with a variety of flowers and the doll is wearing a necklace of glass beads and a cloth bonnet.

The doll was probably a religious figure from a church. It was given to the Musée des Arts Décoratifs in 1923.

DATE
17th or 18th century
NATIONALITY
Italian
AVAILABILITY
rare, expensive
HEIGHT
20½in (52cm)

31 ## PAPIER MÂCHÉ DOLL

A fine doll with papier mâché head and shoulders on a leather body stuffed with bran, and wearing her original dress. She has real hair, plaited in an elaborate style, and fixed glass eyes. She looks rather like a refined version of the doll with the bamboo teeth on page 53, which also has a leather body.

DATE
c1830
NATIONALITY
German
AVAILABILITY
rare, expensive
HEIGHT
19¾in (50cm)

31

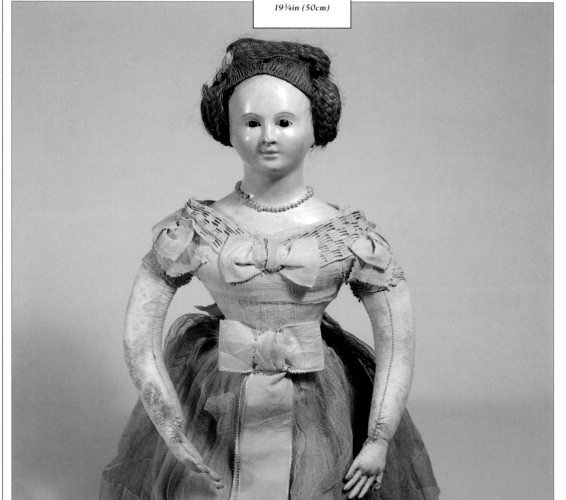

China and Parian

The word china is used by collectors to describe dolls' heads made of glazed porcelain. These were made mostly in Germany from about 1840, but there are also some very desirable Danish heads, made by the Royal Copenhagen factory, and French heads, produced by Huret, Rohmer and Barrois among others, which were the forerunners of the Parisiennes or fashion dolls. The prestigious firms of Meissen and Königliche Porzellanmanufaktur in Berlin are also known to have produced china heads, the latter firm making those that are known for the richness of their glaze and the sensitive modelling of their faces.

The bodies of china dolls vary considerably. Some were sold to shops which supplied them to private buyers for pincushions and other artistic knick-knacks as well as dolls, others were given bodies by outworkers commissioned by the manufacturers. The bodies were mostly stuffed with sawdust and given porcelain or leather lower limbs, but there are many examples of china dolls with wooden bodies.

As well as lady dolls, the early china makers produced boy dolls and some rather fine men, but for some collectors the fascination of this type of doll is in the varied moulded hairstyles of the lady dolls. There were the Queen Victoria dolls with a centre parting and a bun at the back, the braided coronets, the curls surrounding the face, the snoods, the Empress Eugénie style, the bun at the back of the head with ringlets falling from it and many others.

After about 1860 these popular dolls became cheaper and more stylized. A great many Frozen Charlottes were made. These are stiff little white or pink glazed dolls with pillar legs and black moulded hair, the smaller versions of which were used as charms, to be hidden in Christmas puddings and cakes and found by delighted youngsters who, it is hoped, managed to avoid swallowing them.

Later china dolls have a different appearance from the earlier ones. They became more child-like, with chubby faces, short necks and lower foreheads. The sloping shoulders of the early dolls are replaced by smaller, squarer shoulders.

Some blonde china dolls were made, some heads were given a pink lustre finish, others had glass eyes and were made without any hair so that a wig could be added. These dolls often have a black spot painted on the top of the head, though the reason for this is not known.

Another development were the unglazed china dolls, often cast from the same moulds as the glazed dolls. The bisques, as they are called, are usually blonde.

The late 19th century saw the arrival of the bonnet doll, wearing a great variety of headgear in the shape of caps, bonnets, hoods and so on. One fanciful and rather pretty group of these is known as the Marguerites. They wore hats in the shape of apple blossom, butterflies, sham-rock, morning glory and other flowers. Many of these are to be found in the USA, because large numbers of them were exported from Germany to America at about the turn of the century, and they are sometimes collected by enthusiasts.

There were two methods of making glazed china heads. One was to roll out the clay and press it into a plaster of Paris mould; the other way was to mix the clay with water until it was liquid and could be poured. This "slip" was then poured into the mould, where it was left for some minutes until much of the moisture had been absorbed by the plaster. The surplus "slip" was then poured off, leaving a perfect impression. You can tell how a doll's head was made by looking inside it. The pressed mould heads are uneven, because it is difficult to press evenly, while the poured heads are smooth.

The head moulds were usually made in two halves which, when they were "leather hard", were joined together with more "slip". When the whole head was dry, the joins had to be "fettled" so that no line was left to spoil the look of the finished head. (A head mould can also be made in three or more pieces, for a finer finish.) After that, it was a question of bisque-firing the heads and then either painting and overglazing them or glazing them and firing once again with on-glaze enamels.

This process is still used by studio potters to this day, with successful results. Nowadays, studio potters seem to concentrate on either making their own bisque heads or making bisque reproductions of the famous designs of the last century, but in the 1940s a craftswoman named Emma Clear started to make reproduction glazed china dolls, basing her first on an old Jenny Lind doll of the 1850s. Altogether she created about 40 different limited edition dolls during her few working years, each with a cloth body filled with sawdust and with bisque or china arms and legs. Most of them were reproductions and she kept careful records of the donors of the antique dolls from which the master moulds were made. They were copyrighted and patented and they have the Clear name incised on the shoulder with the year of manufacture. Now, of course, these dolls are collector's items in their own right.

Parian dolls

Parian is a form of fine bisque porcelain which derives its name from the island of Paros in Greece, where white marble is found. It is believed that the material was invented by John Mountford of Copeland and it was dearly loved by the Victorians for its resemblance to white marble.

In her book *The Collectors' History of Dolls* Constance Eileen King states that genuine Parian china was used as an expensive medium for minor art objects but was not used for the manufacture of dolls' heads. "The white biscuit porcelain dolls with unglazed faces have been termed 'Parian' by doll-collectors for so long that we may use the term here, although strictly it is incorrect. The fact that the makers of white biscuit heads were aiming at a product that closely imitated the fashionable Parian ware is however inescapable. The doll-makers employed similar decorating techniques, and even constructed shoulder heads that are very reminiscent of busts made to represent famous people."

Whether or not the white bisque dolls we know were true Parian or not, they are attractive to collectors, who have names for them such as Countess Dagmar, Jenny Lind or one of the many well-known ladies of their day, even though they are not portraits. Brenda Gerwat-Clark mentions several in her book *The Collector's Book of Dolls*. There is the blue scarf doll, representing the Empress Louise of Prussia, Miss Liberty, with a lustre crown and streamers, Princess Augusta Victoria and Amelia Bloomer, with painted eyes and short cropped hair. Any of these would make very desirable additions to a collection, even more so if they were given a lustre finish in one of the gold, purple or red colours that were used by the on-glaze decorators.

So-called Parian doll heads, which are usually blonde, were made in Germany from about 1850 to 1880 and were sold without bodies, like the china heads. In fact, some Parians were made from the moulds used for china dolls and they do resemble them. The Colemans have done some research on this and in an article in *Dolls* magazine (August 1992) they showed dolls which were identical in shape and in hairstyle, but which looked quite different because of the light and the dark colouring.

Because they are bisque, the definition of the features of a Parian is more marked than that of the chinas, where the glaze forms a covering surface, obliterating much of the fine detail. The painting of the Parian faces is subtle and attractive and the dolls usually have blue eyes. The bodies vary from the homemade type to the commercially made cloth body with either Parian or leather arms.

Caring for china and Parian dolls

A glazed china doll is as prone to wear and tear as a bisque doll and it should never be scrubbed with harsh abrasives or detergents. If the colour has been added as an on-glaze after the firing of the main transparent glaze, hard rubbing can easily cause the colour, particularly if it is lustre, to disappear. If the colour has been applied as an underglaze, it will be protected by the shiny transparent glaze, but as anyone with a dishwasher knows, even this shiny glaze can be worn away in time.

As with all cleaning, proceed slowly and carefully. Place the doll on a padded surface, such as an old towel. Use a neutral detergent (pure soap flakes) whipped to a foam. Cleaning an inconspicuous area first as a test, use the foam on cotton wool swabs and rinse off with a soft white cloth which has been moistened with warm, distilled water. You can clean Parian and bisque dolls in the same way.

All paint reacts to light, pollution and strong detergents and all china and bisque is liable to damage caused by careless handling and careless placing. It really is best to keep precious china objects safely in a glass case where they cannot be accidentally knocked over.

Collecting china and Parian dolls

It is possible to buy later china and Parian dolls without fancy hairstyles or trimmings, at a reasonable price. Earlier china dolls are more expensive, especially those with fancy hairstyles and glass eyes. Parians with plenty of detailed modelling are also expensive.

In her book *Collecting Dolls* Nora Earnshaw notes that china and Parian dolls are quite easy to find, which signifies that the dolls are, in general, reasonably priced though not cheap, and they could form the basis of a collection.

1

2 GLAZED CHINA DOLL

 A glazed china doll with leather arms and legs and with a different hairstyle. There is a great variety of hairstyles among this type of doll, including braided coronets, waves and curls, buns, loops and centre partings. Most of the German glazed china dolls had brown or black painted hair, painted blue eyes and these sloping shoulders, which looked well in evening dress, though this particular doll is wearing an ordinary brown lace-trimmed dress and a grey striped skirt.

DATE
c1860
NATIONALITY
German
AVAILABILITY
*easy to find,
mid-price range*
HEIGHT
approx 16in (41cm)

1 EMPRESS EUGÉNIE

 A late 19th-century glazed china doll representing the Empress Eugénie of France. She was a noted beauty of her day, with a flair for dressing in glamorous clothes.

Here she is wearing a silk gown, which is trimmed with lace and has a blue embroidered train. She has a complete set of undergarments, including a trimmed and a plain calico petticoat, nun's veiling petticoat, pantalettes and a front-buttoning chemisette.

The white glazed china face has tinted rosy cheeks, and she has painted black hair, painted eyebrows and black painted boots. Her porcelain arms and legs are attached to a pink cloth body and upper limbs. Her ears are pierced to hold earrings.

DATE
c1860
NATIONALITY
German
AVAILABILITY
rare, expensive
HEIGHT
approx 16in (41cm)

3 GLAZED CHINA DOLL II

 Another hairstyle on a glazed china doll with pink cheeks and blue eyes, this time an elaborate coil of hair at the back of the head with falling ringlets. Her arms are of pale leather, her eyes are blue and she is wearing a simple pink dress that shows off her shoulders to advantage. She also has well-shaped ears. Heads were often sold by themselves, the bodies being made by the family or a friendly nanny, but amateurs would not have been likely to attempt a body or limbs of leather. Not many are marked.

DATE
c1860
NATIONALITY
German
AVAILABILITY
*easy to find,
mid-price range*
HEIGHT
approx 16in (41cm)

4 CHINA HEADS

 Two shoulder china doll's heads. On the left is a head with three holes for attaching it to a soft body and 24 ringlets in its moulded hair. The face is confidently painted, with healthy pink cheeks and a red line over the eye to indicate an eyelid.

The doll on the right has only two sewing holes, very sloping shoulders, 10 moulded ringlets and pink cheeks.

DATE
c1870
NATIONALITY
German
AVAILABILITY
*easy to find,
inexpensive*
HEIGHT
*5in and 4in
(12.5cm and 10cm)*

5 PINK LUSTRE CHINA HEAD DOLL

 An early china pink lustre head with pink cheeks and dark brown ringlets. The pink glaze was applied after the colouring to give a rosy glow to the head, a technique used until the 1900s.

The sewing holes are thought to be an indication of the age of a doll, collectors saying that those with three holes are earlier than those with two, but this is not a reliable yardstick and since these heads are unmarked, dating them is largely a matter of guesswork.

DATE
c1840
NATIONALITY
German
AVAILABILITY
*easy to find
inexpensive*
HEIGHT
6in (15cm)

6 CHINA LOWBROW

 Lowbrow glazed china heads became more and more popular towards the end of the 19th century. The shades of blondness varied from honey colour to pale brown and the faces changed, too, becoming more child-like, with very plump cheeks and short necks. Boy dolls were also made, with side partings.

On the left, a doll with wavy hair parted in the centre and low on the forehead. The face is well-painted, with pink cheeks and a red line above the eyes.

DATE
*left, 1890–1900;
right c1880*
NATIONALITY
German
AVAILABILITY
*easy to find,
mid-price range*
HEIGHT
*6in (15cm)
4¾in (12cm)*

7 PINK LUSTRE CHINA HEAD DOLL II

 This pink lustre china-headed doll has a Lacmann-type body – that is, cloth, with leather arms and hands. Lacmann was a contemporary of Greiner and produced bodies for Greiner's papier mâché heads.

The doll has long cloth legs, red leather arms and well-defined hands. She is wearing her original clothing of a long coat over a dress which is trimmed with the coat fabric.

The hair is moulded, with large curls over the ears and a centre parting.

DATE
1860
NATIONALITY
German
AVAILABILITY
*easy to find,
mid-price range*
HEIGHT
16in (41cm)

7

8 AUTOPERIPATETIKOS

 Autoperipatetikos means "walking-about-by-yourself" in Greek, and this is the name the Victorians gave to an automaton doll which did just that, on little metal feet that "walked" beneath its crinoline skirts. China heads were often used on these dolls, with different hairstyles. Here the doll is wearing her hair looped and braided round her head.

She has leather arms and metal feet and is wearing her original dress. The carton base of the doll reads "Patented 15 July 1862 also in Europe 20 Dec 1862", so the maker was taking no chances with his invention.

DATE
c1860s
NATIONALITY
German
AVAILABILITY
rare, expensive
HEIGHT
approx 10in (25.5cm)

9 JENNY LIND

The singer Jenny Lind, known as "The Swedish Nightingale", was popular in Europe and in the USA, where she toured successfully from 1850 to 1851. China head Jenny Lind dolls were made in Germany, and though the singer was a blond, they usually show her with the black wig she wore on stage. In any case, the dolls are idealized portraits.
This particular doll has a lustre finish, porcelain lower arms and legs and a soft body. She is wearing a blue dress and cloak.

DATE
c1850
NATIONALITY
German
AVAILABILITY
easy to find, mid-price range
HEIGHT
15in (38cm)

10 FROZEN CHARLOTTES

DATE
C1890 to 1920s
NATIONALITY
German
AVAILABILITY
easy to find, inexpensive
HEIGHT
½in–18in (1.25–46cm)

These dolls, made all in one piece, with clenched fists and bent elbows, but without any joints, were also known as pillar dolls or bathing babies.
They were usually girls and small, about ½in (1.25cm), 1in (2.5cm) or 2in (5cm) high, though there are some as large as 18in (46cm). The 1in (2.5cm) ones were used in cakes and Christmas puddings as surprise gifts. They were made from the mid-19th century to about 1914.
The name Frozen Charlotte comes from a poem about a vain girl who refused to wear her cloak to the ball because it would have hidden her gown, and who arrived at the ball icily cold.

11 GLAZED CHINA POUPARDE

A doll's head mounted on a stick, which emitted a whistle, squeak or music when it was twirled round. The sound mechanism is concealed beneath the full costume. There are no arms on this doll, which is wearing a blue robe decorated with little bells. It was found in an old sea captain's box of belongings after his death. Perhaps it was intended as a present for a grandchild.

DATE
c1870
NATIONALITY
probably French
AVAILABILITY
easy to find, mid-price range
HEIGHT
13in (33cm)

11

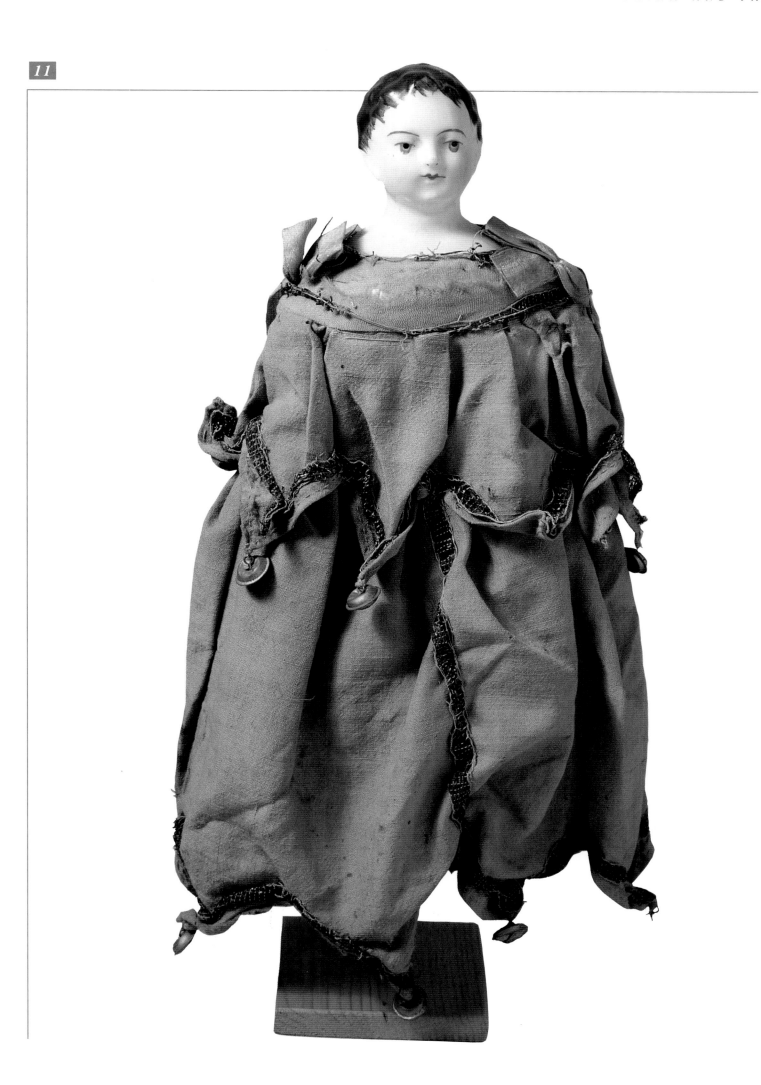

12 COPENHAGEN CHINA

A very lovely Royal Copenhagen china head doll which dates from the 1840s. The production of these heads was limited from c1843 to 1880, with a total production figure of only about 23,000 heads, which were marked with three lines inside the breastplate. The brown-black hair is intertwined into a bun at the centre back of the head and at the back of the exposed ear is a lock of hair ending in brushmarks. The eyes are painted blue and the eyebrows brown. The feet are particularly well modelled. The body is cloth.

DATE
1840s
NATIONALITY
Danish
AVAILABILITY
rare, expensive
HEIGHT
13½in (34cm)

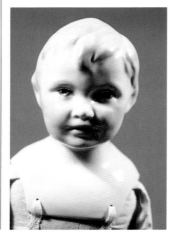

13 EMMA CLEAR DANNY BOY

Emma Clear started her Humpty Dumpty Doll Hospital in Los Angeles in 1917, and began making her china dolls after the Depression years. Mostly they were reproductions taken from moulds of antique dolls but she also made a few originals, among them George and Martha Washington. The American Madonna and this doll, Danny Boy. All Clear dolls made after 1940 have the name incised on the shoulder-plate with the year each one was made and she kept records of the donors of the antique dolls from which she made the master moulds.

DATE
c1940
NATIONALITY
American
AVAILABILITY
rare, expensive
HEIGHT
16in (41cm)

Danny Boy was originally sculpted by Martha Oathout Ayres for Emma Clear. It was a portrait of her son. He has intaglio blue eyes, moulded hair and china lower limbs.

14 EMMA CLEAR ADVERTISEMENT

By 1939 Emma Clear had moved her Humpty Dumpty Doll Hospital to Redondo Beach, California. In that year she advertised her First American China Doll, which was a reproduction of a china shoulder-head with her hair in a bun. The cloth body was corseted, and the lustre shoes had buttons up the sides, high heels and tassels. The doll cost $10 (£6). Emma Clear also sold china and Parian (marble-like white bisque) hands and feet.

15 BONNET HEAD DOLL

A moulded china bonnet head with blue eyes. The brim of the sun bonnet-type hat is orange, there is a blue tie under the chin, and the hat has a pink bow on top. It is marked with a "27". The style of this bonnet for children was made famous by Kate Greenaway in the last quarter of the 19th century.

Bonnet dolls, wearing different styles of hat, were made from about 1860 to 1930.

DATE
probably late 19th century
NATIONALITY
German
AVAILABILITY
easy to find, mid-price range
HEIGHT
2¼in (6cm)

16 MEISSEN **KPM** DOLL

In addition to their usual range of domestic ware, the Meissen factories made dolls' heads of very fine quality during the first half of the 19th century. This one, from Legoland, Denmark, has blond hair and brown eyes, which is unusual. She is by the Königliche Porzellanmanufaktur (KPM) of the Meissen Berlin factory. She is tall, elegant and mature looking, with porcelain lower limbs, and her hair is streaked with a slightly darker colour.

DATE
1840
NATIONALITY
German
AVAILABILITY
easy, inexpensive
HEIGHT
approx 16in (41cm)

17 MEISSEN **KPM** DOLL II

Another glazed china doll from the Meissen KPM factory, Berlin, this time with dark hair and leather lower arms. The colouring of the face of this beautiful doll is particularly subtle. Note how the corners of the eyes are indicated by a red dot, as are the insides of the nostrils. Again, this doll represents a grown woman rather than a child.

DATE
c1837
NATIONALITY
German
AVAILABILITY
rare, expensive
HEIGHT
approx 16in (41cm)

17

18

19 BLOND PARIAN

 An unglazed Parian doll with a stuffed cloth body and china arms and legs, dressed in Russian court dress, consisting of an elaborate black embroidered over-dress, which is laced across the bosom, over a silk and lace under-dress. There is also another layer of petticoat with red fringing, and the doll is wearing a head-dress decorated with beads and sequins. Like many other Parians, she has waved blond hair, tinted cheeks and blue eyes. Some Parian dolls are marked on the inside or on the back of the shoulder-plate. Among the many German manufacturers of this type of doll was the firm of Simon & Halbig.

DATE
c1880
NATIONALITY
German
AVAILABILITY
easy to find, mid-price range
HEIGHT
15½in (39cm)

18 PARIAN DOLL

 The word Parian comes from the name of the island of Paros in Greece, where white marble was found, and this form of fine white bisque porcelain was used for ornaments and statues as well as for dolls from about 1850 to 1880.

This exquisite example has an elaborate moulded hairstyle and hair ribbon, a moulded ribbon round her neck and even a moulded bodice on the shoulder-plate. Because the bisque Parian is fine enough to pick up details from a cast, quite a number of Parian dolls have details of dress moulded into their shoulder-plates.

The doll has leather arms. Her ears are pierced to hold earrings and she has painted blue eyes. Her dress is modern. Parian-headed dolls are generally thought to have been made in Germany, and they are usually blond, the pale yellow showing up well on the white bisque porcelain.

DATE
c1850
NATIONALITY
German
AVAILABILITY
easy to find, mid-price range
HEIGHT
16½in (42cm)

19

20 FORTUNE-TELLING DOLL

Because of its attractive appearance, unglazed Parian was often used for heads on pincushions and other amusements such as "fortune-telling" dolls like this. Known in France as a *poupée bonne aventure*, the doll is wearing a brown lace dress with a mustard yellow trim. Underneath her dress are various leaves of paper in green and white, each with a fortune written on it, such as "Your love is not true" or "Love will come to you".

DATE
1880
NATIONALITY
German
AVAILABILITY
*easy to find,
mid-price range*
HEIGHT
14in (36cm)

21 PARIAN PRINCESS AUGUSTA

A rare and beautiful unglazed Parian doll, the so-called Princess Augusta Victoria, with moulded elaborate hair decorated with a sort of bead tiara, pierced ears and a moulded ruffled collar with a modelled cross. The face painting on Parian dolls is usually of this fine quality. This one has blue eyes like most of her kind, though there are a few brown-eyed Parians about, and some have glass eyes.

DATE
1870
NATIONALITY
German
AVAILABILITY
*easy to find,
mid-price range*
HEIGHT
approx 12in (30.5cm)

22 PARIAN COUNTESS DAGMAR

Countess Dagmar is a Parian doll with finely modelled and detailed hair with plenty of curls. Her blouse, with its high neckline and buttons, also shows this close attention to detail.
She has blue painted eyes with red eye dots and red upper line, a stuffed fabric body, bisque arms and lower legs with black-painted boots, red laces and, unusually, blue painted garters. The dress does not do justice to such a lovely doll, but it was probably made by a child, with whatever fabric was available. Various names are given to different types of china Parian dolls to help collectors identify them for example Alice in Wonderland, Highland Mary, Adelina Patti and, of course, Jenny Lind.

DATE
1870
NATIONALITY
German
AVAILABILITY
*easy to find,
mid-price range*
HEIGHT
17in (42.5cm)

22

23

24 FLORAL DOLL

 A very pretty bisque Parian with moulded flowers, a necklace picked out in lustre and white Parian lower limbs, wearing a white dress with roses and embroidery round the hem. The fair hair is moulded. Although Parian and china dolls are somewhat similar and indeed, it is thought that the white bisque or Parian dolls were often made from the same moulds as the china dolls, the Parian dolls are much more elaborately decorated.

DATE
c1850
NATIONALITY
German
AVAILABILITY
easy to find,
mid-price range
HEIGHT
11in (28cm)

25 PEDLAR DOLL

 A glass-eyed Parian pedlar doll, dressed in a cloak, dress and apron. Her wavy blond hair is parted in the centre and she has leather arms.
She is selling an assortment of objects, including dolls, purses, postcards, gloves, bottles of herbs, beads, laces and buttons.
It is unusual to find a Parian pedlar doll but some craft-minded person must have decided to put her doll to good use and make this model.

DATE
c1850
NATIONALITY
German
AVAILABILITY
easy to find,
mid-price range
HEIGHT
14in (35.5cm)

23 BLONDE PARIAN DOLL

 A rare Parian doll with painted eyes and simply styled blond hair, her head turned to one side. She is quite different from the elegant lady dolls with amazing hairstyles and is a chubby-cheeked, child doll with Parian arms and legs, her feet encased in splendid moulded purple boots.

She came in her original box, with a note fastened to her dress saying "given to my daughter Mary Alice, Oct 9th 1864, the day she was born". Another note reads "ribbon won during the Civil War", so the doll, though German, was exported to America in the middle of the 19th century.

DATE
1864
NATIONALITY
German
AVAILABILITY
easy to find,
mid-price range
HEIGHT
13in (32.5cm)

That she was still there in 1959 is shown by another ribbon which reads "2nd Prize United Federation of Doll Clubs 10th Annual Exhibition Kansas City 1959".

25

Bisque

As mentioned earlier, china-headed dolls were replaced by white bisque (Parian) dolls with white lower limbs and blonde hair. These in turn changed in the 1860s and 1870s into coloured bisque heads of a rounder, more realistic type which were put on the stuffed kid bodies of lady dolls and dressed in the latest Paris fashions of a quality and detail that has to be seen to be believed.

French doll-makers

These matt finish bisque-headed fashion dolls, or Parisiennes as they are called, were a speciality of the French doll-makers, some of which made their own heads while others continued to import the heads from Germany and employed outworkers to make and dress the leather bodies. Jumeau, Rohmer, Huret and Gaultier were among those who made their own heads as well as bodies, but not all are signed. Regardless of who made which bit (and there was a lot of trading among different French companies as well as among French and German companies), a beautifully dressed Parisienne is a prized treasure in any collection. Among the names to look for are those mentioned above and Barrois, Simonne, E. Denamaur, Schmitt & Fils, A. Thuillier, Bru and Jules Steiner. Steiner created dolls with singularly lovely faces.

The firm of Jumeau was established in 1842 by Pierre François Jumeau, with his partner Belton. On Belton's death, Jumeau moved to Montreuil where his son, Emile, built a factory which could undertake all stages of production including making clothes. From 1877, Jumeau was the giant among doll-makers, winning gold and silver medals at international exhibitions.

Jumeau continued to make fashion dolls up to the end of the century and experimented with different types of body, so you could find dolls with bodies of wood covered with leather, all-wood with a bisque head, filled with cork or horsehair, and with or without a swivel neck. Limbs were made of leather, wood or porcelain.

Jumeau also made a completely different type of doll named the bébé, which represents a child about eight years of age. It is not thought that the company invented this new doll, for though Jumeau was the driving force behind the French doll industry, the bébé had been made quite early on by Jules Steiner and Bru and advertised by manufacturers in the 1850s.

With the bébé came a different type of body. Instead of the gusseted kid leather body stuffed with sawdust, bodies were made of wood and ball-jointed, which made them rather expensive. Later, they were made of composition, which lowered the cost. Bébés were in general circulation by the 1870s and were tremendously popular; by 1881 it is said that Jumeau had sold 85,000 of them.

The French firm of Bru was a competitor of Jumeau. Founded by Léon Casimir Bru in 1866, it was always a leader in innovation and quality – its aim was to make high quality dolls, so its output was smaller than that of Jumeau. Among its innovations were double-faced dolls, walking and talking dolls, and one called Le Dormeur, which could open and close its eyelids.

Early Bru dolls have pink or white kid bodies and articulated porcelain or wooden limbs. The bébés have very lovely, finely modelled faces, swivel necks on a shoulder plate and a cork pate and they are marked with a crescent and circle or sometimes with a circle and dot. Some later Bru dolls have wooden, ball-jointed arms and legs.

F. G. Gaultier is another maker of fine bisque heads, who built a porcelain factory in Saint Maurice in 1867. He patented a method of cutting out and inserting glass eyes in bisque heads. His heads were often bought and used on different bodies by other firms, including Simonne and Rabery & Delphieu.

The Lanternier factory of Limoges made some lively looking bisque-headed dolls, but of varying quality.

By the end of the 19th century, German doll-makers had perfected their mass-production methods and were exporting cheap but strong dolls with jointed composition bodies and bisque heads. In order to combat this growing competition, in 1898 French doll-makers (Jumeau, Bru, Fleischmann & Bloedel, Rabery & Delphieu and Godchaux and in 1899 Gaultier) forsook their former rivalries in the face of the enemy, joined together and formed the SFBJ, or Société Française de Fabrication de Bébés et Jouets.

Moulds previously used by the individual members of the company were re-used so there is a strong resemblance between SFBJ dolls and early Brus, Jumeaus and so on. In fact, a marked SFBJ doll may also have a Jumeau or other maker's stamp on it. SFBJ also used German heads on some of its dolls but a great many of the heads continued to be made in the SFBJ factories, which had an output of several millions a year by 1922. This prolific production means that collectors today can still buy a wide range of SBFJ dolls of every sort and every quality.

German doll-makers

Some of the French firms were able to make every part of a doll in their own factories but in Germany, where there were many small firms making dolls, there was interchange of heads and parts among the various manufacturers.

During the fewer than a hundred years from the middle of the 19th century to the early part of the 20th century, German doll-makers dominated the world market. Situated for the most part in the district of Thuringia in southern Germany, where there were natural resources of wood and china clay and plenty of labour, they clustered together, exchanging ideas, making good use of each others' skills, even intermarrying. They were also well organized. Mass production was carried out on an assembly-line basis, one set of workers making wigs, another set of girls making clothes and so on, all usually for very low wages. A large proportion of this output was exported and most of the world's children played with German dolls and toys until World War I.

The firm of Armand Marseille was the most prolific of all German doll-makers. It established a porcelain factory in 1885 and continued production, under the direction of Armand's son Hermann, until the 1950s. Because of its high rate of production its dolls can be found easily by collectors and at a reasonable price. Among its huge range of dolls (which are usually marked "A.M." and/or "Armand Marseille" and "Germany") were its Dream Babies, Flora-doras, googly-eyed dolls and orientals. Like many other doll manufacturers, Armand Marseille supplied heads to other firms, including Cuno & Otto Dressel.

After the little girl dolls came the fashion for baby dolls, with baby-like faces, and bent-limbed bodies and character dolls, which resembled real babies but which were not always pretty, with crying, laughing, sulky faces and so on.

From 1886 to 1909, the firm of Kammer & Reinhardt had made only dolly-faced dolls, claiming to be the first to put teeth into doll's heads, though this seems unlikely. Then, inspired by the realism of the New Art Dolls of Munich, it made the first of its long line of character dolls. These became enormously popular and put new life into the flagging German doll industry at the beginning of the 20th century.

The Kammer & Reinhardt dolls are very appealing. The best known models are the so-called Kaiser baby (though it was not actually modelled on the infant Kaiser), those made in mould 101, known as Peter and Marie, and the Hans and Gretchen dolls, the models for which, say the Colemans, were Reinhardt's grandchildren.

Simon & Halbig was another long-established Thuringian porcelain manufacturer and a prodigious maker of good quality doll's heads, second only in size to Armand Marseille. A great many German doll-makers and some French ones, including Jumeau and other members of the SFBJ, used Simon & Halbig heads from about 1900 and its range of

heads was vast. There are dolls with moulded hair, shoulder-heads, socket heads, doll's house doll heads, dolls with sleeping eyes, brown heads, character heads and many others. Its bisque shoulder-heads are among the earliest marked dolls to be found.

The firm of J. D. Kestner was the only German doll manufacturer to make both heads and bodies and one of the first to make dressed dolls. Founded in 1816, it produced papier mâché and wooden dolls, acquiring a porcelain factory in 1860 and making glazed porcelain doll's heads. Its dolls are considered to be of the highest quality.

More confusion surrounds the name of Heubach, since there were two doll-makers working at about the same time, Gebrüder Heubach of Lichte and Ernst Heubach of Koppelsdorf. The son of Armand Marseille had married the daughter of Ernst Heubach and in 1919 the porcelain factories of Marseille and Heubach merged to become the Koppelsdorfer Porzellanfabrik, making doll's heads, many of them for other firms. Gebrüder (the brothers) Heubach also made some good-looking dolls of different types, with socket or shoulder-heads, and with moulded hair or wigs.

A Schoenau & Hoffmeister doll can be confused with a Simon & Halbig, because the companies had the same initials. Both used a star mark on some of their heads; heads made by Simon & Halbig for Kammer & Reinhardt, for example, sometimes have a star with a K and R on either side and the "S & H" underneath. Schoenau and Hoffmeister also sometimes have a star with a "PB" in the centre and the initials S and H on either side. (The PB stands for Porzellanfabrik Burggrub.) Both firms supplied dolls' heads to other makers.

The Handwercks (Max and Heinrich), Cuno & Otto Dressler, Fritz Bartenstein, Theodor Recknagel, Hermann Steiner and Kley & Hahn are just a few of the dozens of German doll manufacturers that were supplying dolls to the world during the second half of the 19th century and the first years of the 20th.

British ceramic dolls

British bisque dolls have not been highly rated in the past but there are some worth collecting if only for their interest value. World War I cut off the supply of German bisque dolls and the Staffordshire potteries were encouraged to make "pot" dolls to fill the gap in the market, out of an inferior type of clay, usually known as British ceramic, often using moulds made from existing German dolls. Perhaps this is why the English dolls seen in photographs all look very much alike.

By 1917 about 100 factories were producing dolls in the UK, though not on a large scale. They had British ceramic heads and bodies of white kid, cloth or composition. Towards 1918 there was quite a shortage of ceramic heads because the firms regarded doll-making as a sideline, giving priority of firing to their usual lines of domestic pottery.

The Diamond Pottery Co. Ltd. of Hanley, Staffordshire, was one such company, producing some heavy doll's heads of pinkish hue, and the Doll Pottery Co. of Fenton, Staffordshire, also made a variety of dolls and dolls' heads. Again, there can be confusion with these initials.

W. H. Goss of Staffordshire made Parian dolls in the 19th century. During World War I it produced bisque-headed dolls with heavily painted faces and either painted or glass eyes.

Hancock & Sons and Hewitt & Leadbeater of Longton, Staffordshire (manufacturers of porcelain crest china), were among those that joined the other pottery firms in making dolls at the outbreak of the war.

Nunn & Smeed of Liverpool made jointed dolls with a new finish for bodies that looked like porcelain and was waterproof and non-toxic. In 1921 the company took out a patent for the Nunsuch walking doll, which had a composition head, papier mâché arms and legs and spring hinges at the knees. It also made some good-looking Dolly Dimple dolls with British ceramic heads coated with wax.

W. Speight of Dewsbury began business making hair pieces and theatrical wigs, but went on to make dolls after the outbreak of war in 1914. By 1920 it was advertising all kinds of ceramic-headed dolls such as Dinkie, Dazzle Dazzle and Kidette Classic fully jointed dolls.

American bisque doll makers

American firms such as Horsman and Borgfeldt imported quantities of dolls from Germany and France but they also commissioned American artists to design dolls for the American market. The Horsman Campbell Kids were inspired by advertising characters for soup of that name and their HEbees and SHEbees were based on drawings by Charles Twelvetrees.

Borgfeldt commissioned designer Grace Drayton, who is known best for her googly-eyed dolls, to design dolls for him and also Grace Storey Putnam, who created the famous Bye-Lo Baby, the Million-Dollar Baby. Grace Storey Putnam modelled this doll from a real-life baby which she found after a long search and it was a huge commercial success, selling in thousands. The heads were made by several different German doll manufacturers.

Caring for bisque dolls

The same rules apply to cleaning bisque dolls as for cleaning china dolls. The paint on a doll's face may have been fired on but it is still vulnerable to harsh treatment. In some cases, the colour may not have been fired on and then it is even more important not to wash with harsh detergents or to scrub.

Work slowly and carefully. As with china, when cleaning bisque, test a small, inconspicuous area before you begin to work on the whole doll and if the colour "lifts", stop at

once. Cover the body of the doll with a plastic bag to protect it from the moisture. Remove the hair if this is possible without causing damage or lift it away from the face and pin it up.

Whip some neutral detergent into a foam and use the foam on cotton wool swabs to clean the face. Rinse off with a soft white cloth which has been dampened with distilled water. Use cotton wool buds for ears, nostrils and eye corners. If there are any hairline cracks, remove the dirt with moist cotton wool, working along with the length of the crack.

Collecting Bisque dolls

Because they produced so many of them, SFBJ (French) dolls are within the price range of the average collector; Jumeau and Bru are among the more expensive.

Among the German dolls, Armand Marseille are a reasonable purchase; rare character dolls are in the upper price bracket. As explained before, it is possible to become very confused by the different German manufacturers, which exchanged heads and marks with abandon. It is always advisable to familiarize yourself with the makers' marks before buying any doll, but particularly so with a German one.

English bisque dolls are interesting and still available to most collectors, but English manufacturers did not make fine bisque. The finest English dolls are, of course, made of wax.

American bisque dolls are not often found in Europe but a Bye-Lo Baby can be found in the USA for a reasonable sum.

A great many amateurs are now making reproduction antique dolls using moulds cast from original dolls by the top makers of the past. Provided they are signed and dated, there is nothing wrong with this and some collectors like them, but there are also many excellent doll-artists working in porcelain in Europe and in America who are making original dolls of the finest quality. These craftspeople usually produce limited editions especially for collectors and one can be sure when buying them that they will be of value in the future.

1 PARISIENNES

Dolls resembling fashion models, with adult faces and figures, are known as Parisiennes by collectors, and these two dolls are a wonderful evocation of an age of elegance which has long since gone.

Parisiennes came into being in the 1860s, a period when women's fashions were extremely elaborate and complicated, and every sort of ruffle, pleat, button, ribbon or frill was introduced on creations for the affluent. These two Parisiennes in their original costumes are typical of their kind. The doll in the white dress has a fixed, unmarked head in chubby-cheeked Huret style and, as was usual on this type of doll, a hand-sewn, gusseted kid body.

The dress belonged to the trousseau of the other doll, which is marked on the chest "Simonne 1 à 13 Passage Delorme, Rue de Rivoli, Paris" and on the head "F.G.", the initials of Fernand Gaultier, a well-known doll-maker whose heads are often found on Jumeau bodies. The house of Simonne existed from 1839 to 1878, and it is thought that it bought doll parts from other firms and dressed them. There is no record of the Simonne mark on a doll head, and heads on Simonne dolls vary from doll to doll.

DATE	*1860s*
NATIONALITY	*French*
AVAILABILITY	*rare, expensive*
HEIGHT	*approx 18in (46cm)*

1

2 UNMARKED FASHION DOLL

This unmarked fashion doll is probably a Jumeau. She has a swivel head on a bisque shoulder-plate, a leather body and arms that end in well-defined leather fingers. She is sitting down and has fixed blue glass eyes. Her two-piece costume is buttoned down the front to open over a full, pleated skirt of the same fabric.

DATE	*c1870*
NATIONALITY	*French*
AVAILABILITY	*rare, expensive*
HEIGHT	*20½in (52cm)*

3 GAULTIER FASHION DOLL

A doll marked "F.G.4", the initials of Fernand Gaultier, with bisque swivel head and shoulder plate and leather gusseted body. Her wig is made of real hair.

The Gaultier company worked in Paris between 1860 and 1916, and Fernand Gaultier exhibited dolls' heads at the Paris Exhibition in 1878, when he was awarded a silver medal. The company was awarded many more medals from then until 1900. They supplied other doll-makers with heads as well as making dolls themselves.

DATE	*c1870*
NATIONALITY	*French*
AVAILABILITY	*rare, expensive*
HEIGHT	*17½in (44.5cm)*

3

4

4 PARISIENNES II

Two more Parisennes in smart walking outfits. The one on the left is wearing a green silk dress trimmed with black and a lace half-bonnet. She has a wool wig and white kid arms on a stuffed stockinette body and she has a swivel neck.

The other doll is wearing a white dress trimmed with red and a red bonnet tied on with black ribbon. She, too, has white kid arms, and both dolls have fixed blue eyes. Dressed dolls like this reflected the very latest in Paris fashion and were sold complete with a full complement of underwear and accessories.

DATE
1860
NATIONALITY
French
AVAILABILITY
rare, expensive
HEIGHT
16in (40.5cm);
15in (38cm)

5 JOINTED DOLLS

Two finely made, jointed dolls made of turned wood covered with leather. The bisque head is of German origin, though unmarked.

They are identically clothed except for bows and ribbons, pink on one, blue on the other. They were packed in a box with the trademark of Wilhelm Simon and the name "Maquette".

They were long believed to be French because of their French name, but in fact Wilhelm Simon worked in Hildburghausen, Germany, and produced dolls in competition with the well-known Sonneberg toy firms.

DATE
1870
NATIONALITY
German
AVAILABILITY
rare, expensive
HEIGHT
18in (46cm)

6 BRU DOLL

A Bru doll with fixed glass eyes and closed mouth. This is not a fashion doll, but a bébé, a doll representing a child of about 10 years old, often stylized, with large eyes and perfect features. Introduced by the French to compete with German manufacturers, they were a development from the Parisiennes, which were still being sold well into the 1880s. Towards the end of the century, when the bébés were made with composition bodies and were therefore less expensive, they became more popular.

This bébé has fixed eyes, a closed mouth and a composition body. She is wearing her original lace-trimmed dress with a sash.

DATE
c1890
NATIONALITY
French
AVAILABILITY
easy to find,
mid-price range
HEIGHT
28in (71cm)

5

6

7 PARISIENNES III

Three fashionably-dressed Parisiennes with swivel heads and blue eyes. The one on the left in the pale lilac dress has leather arms and is a Jumeau; the doll in the centre is a Fernand Gaultier doll, with "F.G.6" impressed on the shoulder-plate and head; the doll in the maroon dress is impressed "L. déposée 1d" on the shoulder-plate.

The two last dolls have soft bodies but appear to have composition hands. They are all in immaculate condition.

DATE
c1870
NATIONALITY
French
AVAILABILITY
rare, expensive
HEIGHT
15in (38cm)
22½in (57cm)
14½in (37cm)

8 BRU WITH BONNET

A Bru bébé dressed in elaborate child's clothing. She has brown eyes, an open/closed mouth and a blond mohair wig. Her head is incised "Bru Jne 9" and she is also incised on her shoulder-plate.

She has a swivel head, kid body, bisque lower arms and wooden lower legs.

DATE
c1880
NATIONALITY
French
AVAILABILITY
rare, expensive
HEIGHT
20in (51cm)

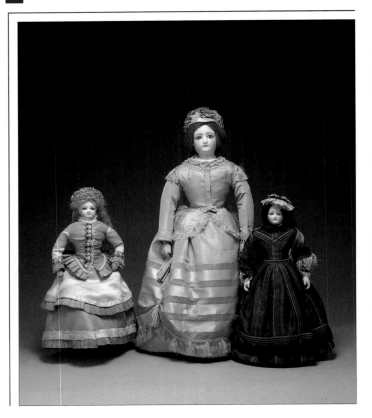

9 SFBJ CHARACTER DOLL

An SFBJ (Société Française de Fabrication de Bébés et Jouets) character doll, impressed "SFBJ 250 Paris 1 SO", with open mouth showing upper teeth, a dimple in her chin, weighted, blue glass flirty eyes, pierced ears and an auburn real hair wig. She has a jointed wood and composition body and is wearing a smart navy blue sailor suit, which was made by the former owner, using old fabrics. She is wearing a pair of long leather boots.

DATE
c1910
NATIONALITY
French
AVAILABILITY
rare, expensive
HEIGHT
22½in (57cm)

10 SFBJ DOLL

This SFBJ doll is wearing a costume that was the height of fashion in 1925, and the doll probably dates from then, as the SFBJ (Société Française de Fabrication de Bébés et Jouets) was producing millions of dolls at its eight factories in that year.

The SFBJ was formed in 1898 to compete with the successful German doll trade. Bru and Jumeau were among the manufacturers in the syndicate, which continued to produce dolls well into the 1930s. This doll has a bisque head and a composition body, a swivel neck and an open mouth showing four teeth.

DATE
c1925
NATIONALITY
French
AVAILABILITY
easy to find,
mid-price range
HEIGHT
20in (51cm)

11

11 COSTUME FIGURES

Two bisque Parisienne-type dolls with kid bodies and arms and blue eyes, dressed in French regional costume. They probably represent a bridal couple.

The bridegroom is wearing a brown jacket over a cream waistcoat fastened with white pompoms and knee breeches. His hat is decorated with ribbons.

The bride is wearing a dress with a gold brocade top, a yellow skirt and a red jacket. Her head-dress is made of lace, and she has a wreath of flowers in her hair and more flowers at her waist.

DATE
1870s
NATIONALITY
French
AVAILABILITY
rare, expensive
HEIGHT
10¼in (26cm)

12 BISQUE JUMEAU DOLL

A fine long-faced Jumeau with open/closed mouth, a new fair curly wig and fixed blue eyes. This bébé has composition arms and legs and is wearing a cream coat trimmed with cream fur over a cream wool dress. Formerly in the Mechanical Music and Doll collection, Chichester, this doll was one of many stolen in March 1992.

The long-faced Jumeau dolls are also known as Jumeau Triste dolls, as their faces are more elongated than usual and have a somewhat sad expression. The Jumeau Triste face is often found on bodies marked "Médaille d'Or", and it was frequently used with ball-jointed Jumeau dolls with fixed wrists.

DATE
1870s
NATIONALITY
French
AVAILABILITY
rare, expensive
HEIGHT
24in (61cm)

12

13

13 JUMEAU DOLL

This charming doll which is probably an unmarked Jumeau, is wearing a cream silk bridal dress and a bridal wreath in her blond hair.

The firm of Belton and Jumeau was producing dolls in 1842 and Pierre Jumeau retired in 1877, handing over to his son, Emile. During Emile's time, the firm was awarded five gold medals and a silver medal at international exhibitions.

Certainly, this doll with a bisque head, hands and arms, kid body and blue glass eyes has the hallmarks of a fine quality Jumeau. She has clearly defined eyebrows, a neat, closed mouth and a beautifully painted face. Her dress is also of the quality associated with a Jumeau Parisienne.

DATE
late 19 century
NATIONALITY
French
AVAILABILITY
rare, expensive
HEIGHT
approx 12in (30cm)

14 SPEAKING DOLL

The Jumeau bébé talking doll was put on the market in the mid-1880s. It worked by pulling two strings which set in motion an uncomplicated voice box hidden in the body. Later in the 19th century Jumeau made dolls incorporating the newly invented phonograph.

This particular talking Jumeau has sleeping eyes, a composition body and an open mouth showing teeth. She is wearing her original white silk dress. She also has the marks "Bébé Jumeau Diplôme d'Honneur" on her body and "Tête Jumeau" on her head.

DATE
1870s
NATIONALITY
French
AVAILABILITY
rare, expensive
HEIGHT
20in (51cm)

15 LONG-FACED DOLL

A large, long-faced Jumeau Triste bébé with dark blue eyes, a bisque head and open/closed mouth. She has a dimple in her chin and earrings in her pierced ears. Her body is made of semi-jointed composition, as are her arms. The wrists are fixed. She is wearing a white dress with white embroidery at the neck.

DATE
c1880
NATIONALITY
French
AVAILABILITY
rare, expensive
HEIGHT
34in (85cm)

14

15

16 E. ROCHARD DOLL

DATE
1867–77
NATIONALITY
French
AVAILABILITY
rare, expensive
HEIGHT
26in (64cm)

This rare bisque-headed doll with a kid body, wooden arms and pale complexion is signed by Ed. Rochard. Apart from the fact that she is a very beautiful doll, the necklace she is wearing is of great interest. It consists of 22 convex glass insets or "Stanhopes", each of which contains a tiny photograph. Stanhopes were named after their inventor, Charles, 3rd Earl of Stanhope. They are actually lenses into which photographs have been embedded and they are inserted into holes in the bisque shoulder-plate where they are glued in place.

To see the photographs, the doll has to be held up to the light at a certain angle, when they catch the light coming from a cut-away section at the back of the shoulder plate. When the eye is placed to the convex surface of the jewel, the lens magnifies the photographs. Edmond Rochard took out a 15-

year patent for Stanhopes in 1867, intending them to be inserted into dolls, toys and religious objects to make them more attractive.

The doll has slightly parted lips to allow for the viewing of a kaleidoscope inside the doll's head, which was to be hidden by the hair.

The photographs in the necklace are of places of tourist interest in Paris, Geneva and Venice, with the addition of six religious scenes in the cross. These photographs enable the doll to be dated between 1867 and 1877, but although the doll is signed by Ed. Rochard, there is no record of any doll-maker of that name and could be by any one of several well-known French manufacturers of that period.

There is another Rochard doll in the Margaret Woodbury Strong Museum, New York, and two others were sold at Sotheby's in 1982.

17 E. DENAMUR DOLL

A bisque-headed doll with jointed composition body and open mouth showing teeth, marked "E 11 D" and probably made by E. Denamur, who made dolls in Paris from 1867 to 1898. Unfortunately for collectors, there were two other doll-makers with the same initials, E. Dumont and E. Daspres, which makes identification more than usually difficult.

DATE
c1910
NATIONALITY
French
AVAILABILITY
rare, expensive
HEIGHT
20in (51cm)

18 SCHMITT ET FILS DOLL

A closed mouth bébé with a bisque head, blue glass eyes, lambswool hair and ball-jointed composition body.

In the hollow of her head are the markings "SCH3". Schmitt et Fils were based in Paris from 1863 to 1891. The company advertised its indestructible jointed bébé, called Bébé Schmitt, in 1879, about the same time that Jumeau and other French companies were bringing out their child dolls. The big eyes, rosebud mouth and chubby chin are hallmarks of the firm, as are the dolls' flat bottoms, which enable them to sit easily.

DATE
late 1870s
NATIONALITY
French
AVAILABILITY
rare, expensive
HEIGHT
19in (48cm)

19 HURET DOLL

An unusual male doll, complete with beard and moustache, which is marked on the back "Huret, rue de la Boetie". The wig is not original. The body is made of jointed wood and the hands are metal.

This doll and its companion are shown in a scene entitled "Chez Alfred de Musset". The poet was not married, so the bisque-headed fashion doll with the gusseted kid body and blue eyes, dressed in a velvet coat over a yellow satin dress, may just be a visitor. She may also be by Huret, though she is unmarked. She has a swivel head on a bisque shoulder plate, a blonde wig fashioned in a plait round her head, pierced ears from which hang blue earrings and kid hands on which fingers are indicated.

DATE
last half of 19th century
NATIONALITY
French
AVAILABILITY
rare, expensive
HEIGHT
18½in (47cm)
20½in (52cm)

18

20 FASHION DOLL

An unmarked fashion doll with a bisque swivel head and shoulder-plate. Her almond-shaped eyes are blue glass and her arms are of glazed porcelain. Her leather gusseted body enables her to sit easily. Her ears are pierced. Dressed in sombre clothing, she may well be a mourning doll and this is borne out by the black and green cross hanging from her neck.

DATE
last half of 19th century
NATIONALITY
French
AVAILABILITY
rare, expensive
HEIGHT
19¼in (49cm)

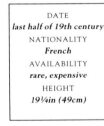

19

21 RABERY & DELPHIEU

A bisque-headed closed mouth bébé by Rabery & Delphieu wearing a fashionable outfit of the late 19th century. She has a jointed composition body. Rabery & Delphieu made dolls in Paris from 1865 to 1898, making lady dolls at first and then bébés with jointed bodies. The firm also tried a few innovations, such as talking dolls that said "Mama" and "Papa" when a string was pulled.

DATE
c1880
NATIONALITY
French
AVAILABILITY
rare, expensive
HEIGHT
14in (35.5cm)

ALSATIAN DOLL

This doll with a bisque shoulder-head, arms and legs and cloth body is dressed in the national dress of Alsace but without the traditional hair ribbon in French national colours. This symbolizes the country's mourning for Alsace, which was annexed by Prussia after France's defeat in the Franco-Prussian war. It was made by Fabrique de Barrois. E. Barrois was a maker and distributor of dolls' heads in Paris from 1858 to 1877. There was also a Madame Barrois who had a shop supplying doll's accessories and who could have been related to the maker.

DATE
c1871
NATIONALITY
French
AVAILABILITY
rare, expensive
HEIGHT
17in (43cm)

23 A. MARQUE DOLL

The model for this rare and lovely doll was made by Albert Marque, a French sculptor who was born in 1872 and died in 1939. Very few of his dolls are known. There are five in the Carnegie Museum, Pittsburgh, USA, and one in the Margaret Woodbury Strong Museum, New York. If one ever appears on the market it is extremely expensive. Marque made many sculptures of children's heads and some dolls, which were sold in Paris. The dolls, which are all the same size, were made from the same mould and have the same composition body with bisque lower arms. They have closed mouths, blue or brown paperweight eyes and an incised signature on the back of the neck.

DATE
c1913
NATIONALITY
French
AVAILABILITY
rare, expensive
HEIGHT
22in (55cm)

This doll has her original wig and her original orange dress with a yellow jacket faced with the same fabric as the dress.

In their book *How to Collect French Bébé Dolls* Mildred and Vernon Seeley (owners of the doll seen here) show a photograph of a terracotta bust of a young girl by A. Marque in the Musée des Arts Décoratifs, Paris, signed and dated 1913. They feel that their Marque doll was made at the same time as the bust, because it is an exact reproduction of it.

24 ORIENTAL DOLL

The firm of Simon & Halbig was one of the largest makers of dolls' heads in Germany in the latter years of the 19th century.

Among the many different types of doll it made were bisque-headed oriental ball-jointed dolls like this one, which is dressed in a robe with a sash. The body is made of composition, the mouth is open to show teeth and the slanting open/close eyes are almond-shaped. The face is delicately tinted and well-painted.

DATE
c1895
NATIONALITY
German
AVAILABILITY
rare, expensive
HEIGHT
17in (43cm)

25 SIMON & HALBIG DOLL

The firm of Simon & Halbig must have produced thousands of bébé dolls of this type, which it exported all over the world. This one has an open mouth with no teeth, a composition jointed body, open/close eyes, swivel neck and is wearing her original wig. Her white lace dress is also original.

DATE
late 19th century
NATIONALITY
German
AVAILABILITY
*easy to find,
mid-price range*
HEIGHT
18in (46cm)

26 SIMON & HALBIG II

This Simon & Halbig doll holding a teddy bear was sold to the Lilliput Museum by the original owner, who had been given the doll when she was three years old. The doll is wearing the white cotton dress with lace inserts given her by the original owner, but it is unlikely that she would have been sold with a dress like this. The doll has a pink leather body, upper and lower limbs of bisque and a swivel neck on a shoulder-plate. She has dark brown fixed eyes, original, real hair and a rather lovely, wistful expression on her face.

DATE
1899
NATIONALITY
German
AVAILABILITY
*easy to find,
mid-price range*
HEIGHT
24in (61cm)

24

26

27 GEBRÜDER HEUBACH DOLLS

The late 19th and early 20th century saw the arrival of a more realistic-looking type of doll, when artists were commissioned by different firms to model the heads. This group shows some typical examples of Gebrüder Heubach dolls.

On the left is a doll with open/closed mouth showing its tongue and a contorted expression on its face, as if crying. The hair is moulded, the body is jointed wood and composition.

In the centre is a laughing doll with bent limbs, open/closed mouth showing two lower teeth, weighted blue glass eyes and a real hair wig.

On the right is a smiling open/closed mouth doll, showing moulded tongue, with moulded blonde hair and a jointed wood and composition body. The intaglio eyes are looking left.

DATE
1912–1914
NATIONALITY
German
AVAILABILITY
easy to find, mid-price range
HEIGHT
largest doll, centre, 14in (36cm)

28

29 ARMAND MARSEILLE DOLL II

This doll was bought as the author's first purchase because of its attractive face and also because it was not too expensive. It is marked "Armand Marseille, made in Germany, DRGM246/1, 390" and has a composition body, with jointed wood and composition arms and legs, which have obviously been repaired and re-strung at some point. Her mouth is open, showing her upper teeth, and she has blue sleeping eyes. She looks very much like the Newhaven fisher girl.

She had no hair at all when she arrived and though this wig is much too large and curly, she looks better with it than she did without it.

DATE
early 20th century
NATIONALITY
German
AVAILABILITY
easy to find, inexpensive
HEIGHT
12½in (32cm)

28 ARMAND MARSEILLE DOLL

The firm of Armand Marseille started to produce dolls in 1865 and was one of the foremost German manufacturers, making a large variety of dolls of varying quality. Most common of all were the "A.M. 390" dolls, which were sold wearing only a simple white shift but which have been dressed in all kinds of ways by their owners.

This one, for example, which is an "A.M. 370" with bisque head and composition body and limbs, blue sleeping eyes and an open mouth showing teeth, is dressed as a Newhaven fisher girl in three petticoats (two striped, one flannel) thick blouse, apron, knitted wool stockings and a red shawl round her neck. Newhaven, near Edinburgh, was an important fishing port and market.

DATE
c1925
NATIONALITY
German
AVAILABILITY
easy to find, inexpensive
HEIGHT
15in (38cm)

29

30 DOLL IN TURKISH COSTUME

A pretty Armand Marseille doll dressed in Turkish costume in a lace dress with a beaded head-dress, her neck decorated with more beads.

Though there are few Armand Marseille so-called character dolls, there are a great many in rather exotic costumes, perhaps because the pretty faces lent themselves to fantasy.

This one has large, dark brown eyes and an open mouth showing teeth. She has a composition body, arms and legs.

DATE
laste 19th century
NATIONALITY
German
AVAILABILITY
easy to find, inexpensive
HEIGHT
12in (30cm)

30

31 ARMAND MARSEILLE DOLL III

An Armand Marseille doll with jointed composition arms, legs and body, open mouth and blue eyes. She is wearing a gown of embroidered broderie anglaise and is holding a small German doll with a bisque head and composition body ("R127A"), which could be an Armand Marseille Dream Baby. Armand Marseille made heads for other German firms, many of which were making baby dolls at the beginning of the 20th century.

DATE
early 20th century
NATIONALITY
German
AVAILABILITY
easy to find, inexpensive
HEIGHT
27in (68.5cm)
9in (23cm)

31

32 CHARACTER BABY

An amusing Kammer & Reinhardt character baby with painted, moulded hair and an open mouth showing its tongue. The body is bent-limbed and has the dimpled knees, creases and rolls of fat seen on real babies. It marks a dramatic change in baby dolls, which became more realistic from this time.

Kammer & Reinhardt was the first German doll manufacturer to try to make a baby doll with an expression on its face.

In 1908, Reinhardt saw the Munich Art Dolls of Marion Kaulitz, dolls with lifelike expressions like real children, and he commissioned a Berlin artist to make Kammer & Reinhardt's

DATE
c1908
NATIONALITY
German
AVAILABILITY
easy to find, mid-price range
HEIGHT
10¼in (28cm)

first baby mould "100". It was an adventurous idea, but new ideas were needed to improve sales, and the character dolls proved to be a tremendous success. The first model was followed by dozens of others. Many heads were made by Simon & Halbig, to Kammer & Reinhardt's specifications.

32

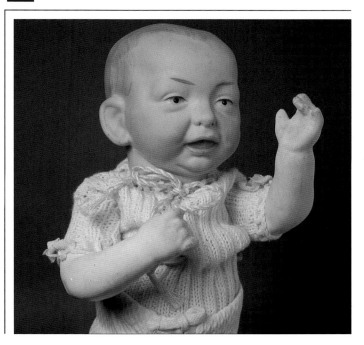

33 GERMAN CHARACTER DOLLS

The two large dolls are by Kammer & Reinhardt. Reinhardt's grandchild was used as the model for the girl (named Gretchen) on the left, whose mould number is 114. Her partner is another Kammer & Reinhardt, named Peter, mould number 101. Both dolls have closed mouths, painted blue eyes and ball-jointed wood and composition bodies.

The winking doll on the left is a rare character doll, probably by Kestner, with bisque head and shoulders and composition body and limbs.

The larger of the two dolls in front is a Hertel, Schwab & Co. googly-eyed doll with curved limbs, composition body and fixed blue eyes, and the small doll in front is a German all-bisque, googly-eyed doll with a smiling mouth.

DATE
two large dolls, 1909;
others 1914
NATIONALITY
German
AVAILABILITY
easy to find,
mid-price range
HEIGHT
from 19¼in (49cm) to
5in (13cm)

34 KESTNER CHARACTER DOLL

A. J. D. Kestner character boy number 142 has a jointed, sawdust-filled leather body and upper arms and legs and composition lower arms and legs. You can just see the unusual jointing of the arms, where the leather meets the composition.

He has painted intaglio eyes, moulded painted hair and an open mouth. He is marked "DRGM 4428107", which means "Deutsches Reichsgebrauchsmuster", the registered design and patent. The clothes are not original.

DATE
early 20th century
NATIONALITY
German
AVAILABILITY
easy to find,
mid-price range
HEIGHT
14in (35.5cm)

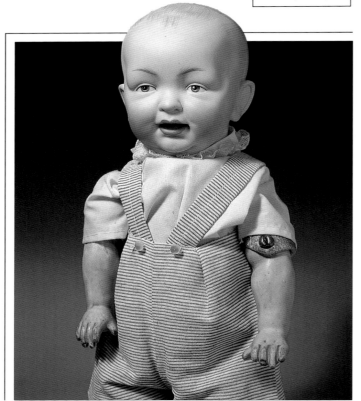

35 ROHMER DOLL

A girl doll by Rohmer of France, famous for its invention of a head that could be turned by pulling a cord running from the head to the body. She has the name Rohmer stamped on her body with a green stamp.

She has a swivel head with a real hair wig, lower arms in glazed porcelain and a leather body. The upper arms and legs are ball and socket jointed wood covered with leather.

She is described as a fashion doll and certainly has the face of one, but here she is dressed in a child's clothes.

DATE
1857–70
NATIONALITY
French
AVAILABILITY
rare, expensive
HEIGHT
20in (51cm)

36

37

36 UNMARKED CREOLE DOLL

 A closed-mouth Creole doll with a brown-tinted bisque head and an unjointed composition body. She is probably a German doll (possibly by Simon & Halbig). Several of the prominent German manufacturers made coloured dolls. They were made from ordinary doll's head moulds, the porcelain tinted to whatever colour skin was required, from Japanese to West Indian.

This good-looking doll is nicely dressed in a brocade and ribbon dress with lace sleeves and lace ruffle at the neck. The ribbon bandeau is particularly appealing.

DATE
about 1914
NATIONALITY
German
AVAILABILITY
*easy to find,
mid-price range*
HEIGHT
14in (35cm)

37 WILLIAM GOEBEL DOLL

 This happy little William Goebel doll with a bisque head, open mouth and bent-limbed composition baby body, is holding a small doll by Hermann Steiner, who is not to be confused with Jules Steiner, a French doll-maker. The small doll has a bisque flange-neck head, closing eyes, closed mouth, a cloth body and composition hands.

William Goebel founded the family firm in 1871 and began producing first porcelain houseware and then, in the 1800s, dolls. The firm also made all-porcelain dolls and supplied other firms with dolls' heads.

DATE
c1910–1915
NATIONALITY
German
AVAILABILITY
*easy to find,
mid-price range*
HEIGHT
*18in (46cm)
7in (18cm)*

38 SCHOENAU & HOFFMEISTER AND SIMON & HALBIG DOLLS

 On the left is a large Schoenau & Hoffmeister doll with a bisque head and jointed composition body wearing her original broderie anglaise dress and cape and a straw hat with swansdown trim. She is holding a small composition doll. Dolls by this German manufacturer are sometimes confused with those of Simon & Halbig, as their initials are the same, though their marks are different.

On the right is a Simon & Halbig doll wearing a white cotton pintucked dress with lace inserts, a white heavily embroidered shoulder cape and a cotton mob-cap.

DATE
c1880s
NATIONALITY
German
AVAILABILITY
*easy to find,
mid-price range*
HEIGHT
*34in (86.5cm)
33in (84cm)*

38

39 PRINCESS ELIZABETH DOLL

 This Princess Elizabeth doll by Schoenau & Hoffmeister is marked "Porzellanfabrik Burggrub", the name of the factory this firm founded to make their bisque doll's heads.

The doll is a portrait of the three-year-old Princess and it was made in 1929. The mould size is 6½, the largest made. The body is that of a straight-limbed toddler, with original mohair wig, blue glass sleeping eyes and open mouth with teeth.

There is an identical version of this doll in the Queen's collection in Windsor Castle.

DATE
1929
NATIONALITY
German
AVAILABILITY
rare, expensive
HEIGHT
24in (61cm)

39

40

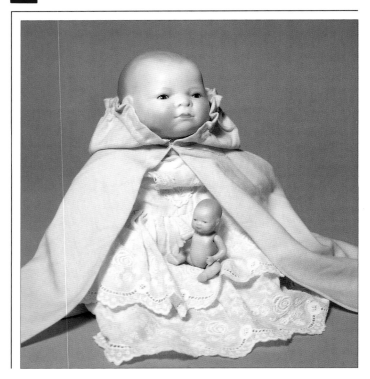

40 BYE-LO BABY

 In 1922 an American art teacher named Grace Storey Putnam designed and copyrighted the Bye-Lo Baby doll for the Borgfeldt Doll Company, Germany. She had searched numerous orphanages and hospitals before finding a suitable child on which to model this doll.

The doll was made with a bisque flanged head, fabric body and celluloid hands. It was an immediate success with huge sales, so much so that it was christened The Million Dollar Baby.

The heads were also made by Kestner, Alt, Beck & Gottschalk and others. The doll

DATE
1922
NATIONALITY
German
AVAILABILITY
easy to find, inexpensive
HEIGHT
13in (32.5cm)

was made in several sizes including the small one seen here, which is all bisque.

41 DPC DOLLS

 There were two English doll-making firms with the initials DPC in the early part of the 20th century. One was the Diamond Pottery Co. Ltd (1908–25), of Shelton, near Hanley, Stoke-on-Trent, and the other was the Doll Pottery Co. Ltd (1915–22) of Fenton, Stoke-on-Trent.

This makes for some confusion when trying to identify the dolls, but those shown above have interchangeable heads marked "D.P.Co." and they are made of stoneware, which is unusual.

The Diamond Pottery Co. made dolls' heads of every sort, in many sizes and prided itself on the natural colouring and expression.

DATE
1916
NATIONALITY
English
AVAILABILITY
easy to find, mid-price range
HEIGHT
4in (10cm)

41

42 | SPEIGHT CLASSIC

Speight, of Dewsbury, Yorkshire, UK, made doll's hair before World War I but started to make dolls in 1916 and by 1920 its Classic range included many different models.

This one has a stoneware head and shoulder-plate, cloth body, composition lower limbs and a mohair wig. She does not compare in quality with German or French dolls.

DATE
c1916
NATIONALITY
English
AVAILABILITY
*easy to find,
mid-price range*
HEIGHT
head 5in (12.5cm)

43 | GOSS DOLL

W. H. Goss & Co. of Staffordshire, UK, made Parian dolls in the 19th century and bisque dolls from about the period of World War I, when German dolls were not available. It also produced baby dolls during World War II. The company's dolls have glass eyes and are rather heavily painted in comparison with the German and French dolls – the red lips and heavy eyebrows of this doll are typical of Goss bisque dolls, which are quite rare. The doll has a bisque head and shoulder plate, fixed eyes and a crude cloth body.

DATE
c1918
NATIONALITY
English
AVAILABILITY
rare, inexpensive
HEIGHT
15in (38cm)

43

44 | UNCLE SAM

DATE
c1896
NATIONALITY
German
AVAILABILITY
rare, expensive
HEIGHT
14in (35.5cm)

Made by Cuno & Otto Dressel in about 1896, this figure of Uncle Sam has a Simon & Halbig bisque swivel head with glasss eyes on a jointed wooden body.

He is wearing his original blue felt top hat, felt jacket, cotton trousers, a vest and a shirt.

At that period, American patriotism was running high because of the Cuban insurrection against Spanish rule, which won the sympathy of many Americans. Cuno & Otto Dressel also produced bisque-headed, composition-body portrait dolls of the Spanish/American war.

There are similar Uncle Sam dolls in the Atwater Kent Museum, Philadelphia, and in the Wenham Historical Museum, Massachusetts, USA.

45

45 ROYAL CHILDREN

The late Martha Thompson's dolls were inspired by literary and historical events. She was fascinated by the British royal family and made a set of dolls representing Prince Charles at four different stages in his childhood. (Queen Elizabeth II has the one-year-old version.) The royal children sold at $25 (£15) each and were made in flesh-coloured bisque. These two, Prince Charles and Princess Anne, which have cloth bodies and bisque lower limbs, were made in honour of the coronation of the Queen in 1953. Among Martha Thompson's other portraits are Mamie and Dwight Eisenhower, Princess Grace and Prince Rainier of Monaco, Princess Margaret and Jacqueline Kennedy.

DATE
c1953
NATIONALITY
American
AVAILABILITY
rare, expensive
HEIGHT
approx 9½in (24cm)

46 BOUDOIR DOLLS

The dolls of Niesje Wolters-van Bemmel of the Netherlands are elegant, beautifully dressed and reminiscent of the boudoir dolls of the 1920s. The heads are made of porcelain bisque from models made by the artist, and they have porcelain lower limbs, attached to fabric bodies. Elbows and knees are left unpadded to allow them to move freely. The clothes of these dolls are made of the finest fabrics, with each frill and button properly sewn into place. The feet are elegantly shod in the appropriate footwear, and the hair is immaculately dressed. The faces are painted in watercolour and varnished.

DATE
1980s
NATIONALITY
Dutch
AVAILABILITY
easy to find, inexpensive
HEIGHT
approx 26in (66cm)

46

47 ROBBIE

Artists Philip and Christine Heath worked as a team for some years making limited edition portraits of children such as this one of Robbie. Philip had been teaching ceramics and Christine was trained in textiles and their dolls were of extremely high quality, with bisque heads and lower limbs and cloth bodies. Now they are working separately, but both are still making high quality dolls. Philip Heath always regarded his dolls as three-dimensional portraits and felt that in making them he was introducing doll lovers to sculpture and art lovers to the doll world.

DATE
1980s
NATIONALITY
English
AVAILABILITY
easy to find, inexpensive
HEIGHT
approx 24in (61cm)

Many Heath dolls, all of which are signed and dated, find their way to the USA where they are eagerly bought by discerning collectors.

47

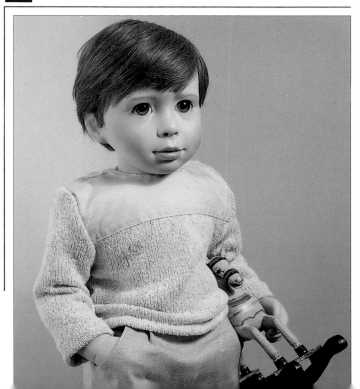

48 GILLIE CHARLSON DOLL

English doll-maker Gillie Charlson created 17 oriental dolls in 1986 for the movie *Shanghai Surprise*, starring Madonna. She had to make the dolls in only five weeks, a task she accomplished by dropping everything else she was doing and working until the small hours of the morning.

She used an oriental head mould and wired the porcelain arms to the body, which was simply a wooden frame on a wooden base, padded to give it shape. The "embroidered" robe was actually painted with textured paint and it hid the fact that the dolls had no legs. The result is very convincing.

DATE
1986
NATIONALITY
English
AVAILABILITY
easy to find, inexpensive
HEIGHT
approx 18in (46cm)

49 REPRODUCTION KESTNER DOLLS

This charming all-bisque reproduction Kestner character baby has bent limbs jointed at hips and shoulders, painted pink nails on his feet and hands and a smiling face. He is beautifully made but too heavy to be a real Kestner and is in any case incised "J. A. 83" on the back. He is wearing a tucked lawn robe, a hand-crocheted vest with buttons and a nappy fastened with a safety pin.

DATE
1983
NATIONALITY
possibly English
AVAILABILITY
rare, inexpensive
HEIGHT
5in (12.5cm)

50 MEIN SUSSER LIEBLING

A Mein Susser Liebling doll with swivel neck on a turned, jointed wood body and limbs. The bodies were made by Kammer & Reinhardt, the firm that eventually took over Simon & Halbig.
The doll has her original blonde wig and is wearing her original clothes.

DATE
c1922
NATIONALITY
German
AVAILABILITY
rare, expensive
HEIGHT
23½in (58.5cm)

51 GOOGLY BISQUE DOLL

Dolls with Googly eyes (also known as roguish eyes) that glance to the side were popular in the 1920s, when they were made by most of the leading manufacturers. This one is marked Strobel & Wilkin, which were importers and agents, so it is likely to have been made by another firm.
The doll has large round fixed glass eyes, a "melon" mouth, moulded and painted hair, composition arms and legs and is wearing 1920s clothing.
When the eyes moved from side to side, they were known as flirting eyes.

DATE
1920s
NATIONALITY
German
AVAILABILITY
easy to find, mid-price range
HEIGHT
7in (18cm)

51

50

52 JULES STEINER DOLL

Not to be confused with the German manufacturer Hermann Steiner, Jules Steiner of Paris, a firm founded in 1855, was famous for the walking Steiner doll, patented in 1890 and other mechanical dolls but it also made some very beautiful open/closed mouth bébés like this one.
The doll has fixed violet eyes, a jointed composition body, pierced ears and is wearing her original wig and clothes.

DATE
1880s
NATIONALITY
French
AVAILABILITY
rare, expensive
HEIGHT
18in (46cm)

53 NUNN & SMEED DOLL

The English firm of Nunn & Smeed of Liverpool made dolls in World War I, when no German dolls were coming into the country, and it continued until it turned to making furniture in 1927.

The jointed dolls had composition bodies with a new type of finish that looked like porcelain and was non-poisonous and waterproof. The company patented a walking doll in 1921 under the name Nunsuch.

Some of the company's dolls had jointed composition arms, legs and bodies with German porcelain heads, so presumably it was either using old stock or, by the 1920s, had begun importing heads again. However, the Dolly Dimple doll, seen here, was advertised as having a British ceramic head, so they made their own heads as well.

When Mr Nunn's son visited the Lilliput Museum on the Isle of Wight, he told the owner that his father had begun his career as a potter and had taken on Mr Smeed as a partner, to make dolls.

DATE
1921
NATIONALITY
English
AVAILABILITY
rare, inexpensive
HEIGHT
16in (41cm)

53

54

54 LARGE BRU

Bru dolls are among the finest of French dolls, beautiful to look at and beautifully made. The bodies were often made of gusseted leather, and they had bisque lower limbs or sometimes carved wooden lower limbs. The swivel heads are well modelled, with slightly parted lips and delicate colour.

Some of the early Bru dolls are marked only with a circle and a dot, like this one, which has a leather body, porcelain hands and leather feet. Her mouth is open/closed that is, the lips are slightly parted and she has fixed blue eyes. She is wearing the original wig, a navy blue velvet dress trimmed with cream lace and a straw hat trimmed with roses.

DATE
c1880
NATIONALITY
French
AVAILABILITY
rare, expensive
HEIGHT
24in (61cm)

55 DPC DOLL

There is some confusion between the owners of the initials DPC. A doll so marked could belong to the Diamond Pottery Company or the Doll Pottery Co., both of which were operating about the same time and in the same area of Staffordshire, UK.

However, this doll with a composition body is marked "Hanley, England", and as the Diamond Pottery Company was situated in Shelton, on the outskirts of Hanley, and the Doll Pottery Co. in Fenton, it seems reasonable to assume that the former firm made her.

DATE
1908
NATIONALITY
English
AVAILABILITY
rare, inexpensive
HEIGHT
17in (43cm)

55

57 HEUBACH DOLL

Gebrüder Heubach, founded in 1820, are famous for character dolls, baby ornaments (piano babies), Easter bunnies and other trivia as well as for dolls. This little Heubach character has a closed mouth, painted intaglio eyes, a composition body and bent limbs. The knitted romper suit is new but the shift is original. There is sometimes confusion between Gebrüder Heubach and another firm founded in 1887 named Ernst Heubach, though their marks are different. The Gebrüder Heubach mark is either a rising sun or "Heubach" in a square.

DATE
c1900
NATIONALITY
German
AVAILABILITY
*easy to find,
mid-price range*
HEIGHT
7in (18cm)

56

56 HANDWERCK DOLL

There were two doll-makers named Handwerck, Heinrich founded his factory near Walterhausen, Germany, in 1876 and Max founded his factory in 1900, also at Walterhausen. Simon & Halbig made bisque heads from Heinrich Handwerck moulds, some of them modelled from life, which were put on Handwerck composition bodies, while William Goebel made the bisque heads from moulds made by Max Handwerck. This Max Handwerck doll, which is marked, has dark brown eyes, an open mouth showing top teeth and a composition body, arms and legs. She is wearing her original dress, a lace bonnet and yellow shoes with bows.

DATE
1902
NATIONALITY
German
AVAILABILITY
*easy to find,
mid-price range*
HEIGHT
27in (68.5cm)

57

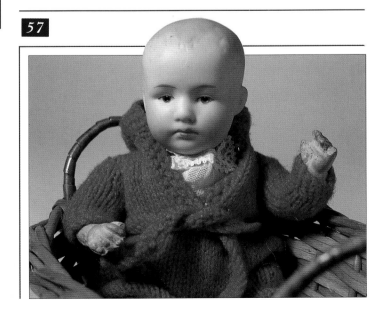

58 FLIRTY EYE DOLL

Many of the major German firms used Simon & Halbig porcelain heads, as did the French – even Jumeau used them. The company made every type of doll's head, with painted eyes, sleeping eyes or, as here, flirting eyes which, moved sideways.

This doll has long, fair hair and an open mouth showing teeth. She is wearing a lawn dress, with knitted socks and a straw hat decorated with flowers.

DATE
1920s
NATIONALITY
German
AVAILABILITY
easy to find, mid-price range
HEIGHT
24in (61cm)

58

59 JOINTED BABY DOLL

A bisque-headed baby doll with moulded hair and painted eyes (mould 100) by Kammer & Reinhardt. The mouth is open/closed and it has a bent-limbed, composition body. Sometimes this model doll has jointed composition limbs and glass eyes.

The firm of Kammer & Reinhardt specialized in character dolls that represented real children in different moods, but the number and type of different dolls the company produced is testimony to its policy of innovation.

DATE
c1913
NATIONALITY
German
AVAILABILITY
easy to find, mid-price range
HEIGHT
13in (33cm)

59

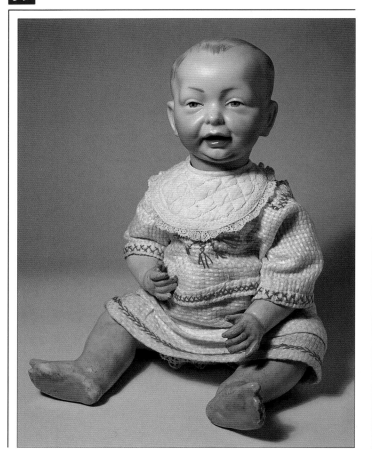

60 KEWPIE DOLL

Kewpie dolls, which are distinguished by their topknots of hair, sideways glance and all-in-one legs, were originally designed by Rose O'Neill, who patented her design about 1913. They were made by Kestner among others, but later they were copied all over the world.

Kewpies started life as a series of drawings for *Ladies' Home Journal* in 1909. Rose O'Neill made a rag doll version of her drawings and Borgfeldt, the agents, asked her to design the Kewpie doll.

Kewpies range in size from about 2½in (6cm) to 17in (43cm), and they come with hair, with eyes looking right or left, coloured black or brown, with wings, without wings, undressed or, like this little fellow, dressed in all kinds of uniform.

DATE
c1920
NATIONALITY
German
AVAILABILITY
easy to find, inexpensive
HEIGHT
3in (7.5cm)

60

61 MAROTTE

The firm of Ernst Heubach of Koppelsdorf, Thuringia, made quite a wide variety of dolls at its porcelain factory. Like most German makers, it made heads for other firms, including Cuno & Otto Dressel. This marotte or doll on a stick is marked with the distinctive horse-shoe mark of Ernst Heubach.

A marotte is swung round on its stick to start a musical movement hidden under the costume. The bells add to the sound. Some marottes, like this one, have a squeaker instead of music. There seems to be little difference between a marotte and a pouparde; both are heads on sticks with some kind of music, whistle or squeaker hidden under the clothing.

DATE
c1900
NATIONALITY
German
AVAILABILITY
easy to find, mid-price range
HEIGHT
13in (33cm)

61

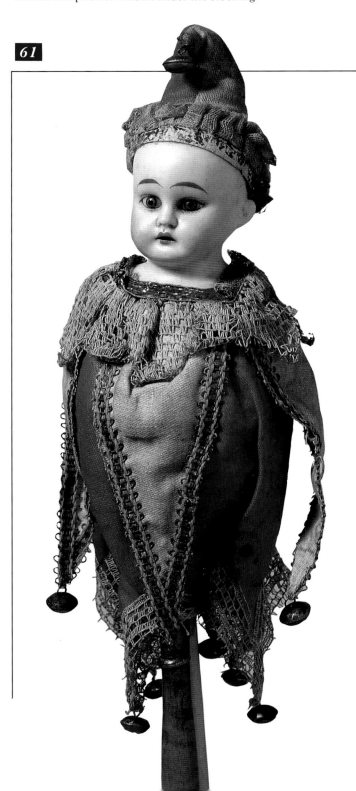

62 MY DREAM BABY

The Armand Marseille My Dream Baby was one of the firm's most popular baby dolls, which was made up until the 1930s, in a wide range of sizes. This one, which is marked "A.M. 341–6K", has a closed mouth, composition body, bent limbs and blue sleeping eyes. It is wearing its original clothes.

DATE
c1920
NATIONALITY
German
AVAILABILITY
easy to find, mid-price range
HEIGHT
18in (46cm)

63 DEP DOLL

This small boy doll is marked "D.E.P. R/A Recknagel 1907". The initials DEP stand for *Deponiert* and indicate that the design was registered. The firm of Theodor Recknagel had a factory at Alexandrienthal, where it made bisque heads.

The doll has an open mouth with teeth, fixed eyes, a straight-limbed body jointed at hips and shoulders, a swivel neck and a composition body. He is wearing a felt jacket, lace shirt, velvet trousers and painted shoes. He has his original hair.

DATE
1907
NATIONALITY
German
AVAILABILITY
easy to find, mid-price range
HEIGHT
6in (15cm)

63

64 LIMOGES DOLL

"Favorit no 2" was designed by the sculptor J. E. Masson, who made models of wax and clay for art dolls. The bisque dolls' heads were made in Limoges by Lanternier & Cie. and by Couty, Magne & Cie. The doll has the Masson signature and "A. L. & Co" on the neck.

This character doll, which has been re-wigged and re-dressed, has fixed eyes, heavily painted eyebrows, a dark red open mouth showing upper teeth and holes in her ears for earrings. She has a jointed composition body and limbs.

DATE
1915
NATIONALITY
French
AVAILABILITY
rare, expensive
HEIGHT
16in (41cm)

64

65 LYNNE AND MICHAEL ROCHE DOLL

After a period of making reproduction antique dolls, the first doll that Lynne and Michael Roche of Bath, UK, made was based on a photograph of the French writer Colette as a child. That was in 1982, since then they have made many other models of fine, timeless, quality with bisque heads and bodies and more recently, with jointed wooden bodies.

Michael is in charge of mould-making and body-making while Lynne is in charge of the clothes. They work on the heads together.

All the dolls are marked on the head and on the body with the copyright date, the name of the doll, its number and the names of the makers.

Members of the British Toymakers Guild, the Roches attend American and German toy fairs, where they are well known for their "strong and unsentimental images" of children in porcelain and wood.

This doll, Sophy, is made in several sizes, one of which is an all-bisque 12in (30cm) doll. The 23in (58.5cm) size seen here is in a limited edition of 100. She has a ball-jointed wooden body and porcelain hands.

DATE
1990s
NATIONALITY
English
AVAILABILITY
easy to find, inexpensive
HEIGHT
23in (58.5cm)

65

66

66 SIMON & HALBIG DOLL

This charming doll by Simon & Halbig is dressed in clothes of 1880. She is wearing a smart two-piece dress with a small bustle, a matching hat and gold leather boots with heels.

The doll has blue glass eyes and is wearing a blond wig. Her ears are pierced and she has bisque arms on a soft body. She is marked "S 6 H".

DATE
c1880
NATIONALITY
German
AVAILABILITY
easy to find, inexpensive
HEIGHT
15½in (40cm)

67 GIRLS' BRIGADE DOLL

This charming little Armand Marseille bisque doll with a composition body is dressed in the uniform of the Girls' Brigade. The navy blue skirt symbolizes loyalty and the white blouse, purity.

Probably German, she has blue sleeping eyes and is wearing her original wig.

DATE
c1927
NATIONALITY
German
AVAILABILITY
easy to find, mid-price range
HEIGHT
15in (38cm)

68 PROVINCIAL GERMAN DOLL

The major German firms made costume dolls of nearly every country in the world, dominating the market until 1914.

The brown-eyed, open-mouthed Armand Marseille Floradora, with composition arms and legs, is wearing a traditional provincial German costume, with a black embroidered dress open to show a striped petticoat. On her head she is wearing a lace cap.

DATE
c1900
NATIONALITY
German
AVAILABILITY
easy to find, mid-price range
HEIGHT
18in (46cm)

68

69 JAPANESE DOLLS

Dolls have been part of Japanese culture for centuries. They were part of the Japanese Girls' Doll Festival celebrations held every year on 3 March, when dolls were placed on five red steps to symbolize the Emperor and Empress, their ladies-in-waiting, sentinels and coolies, models of household utensils and refreshments for visitors. The Boys' Festival was on 5 March, and their dolls represented famous warriors.

During the early part of the century, Japanese dolls were imported by large department stores in Europe and America.

There is a distinction between Japanese dolls made in Japan, western imitations of Japanese dolls, and Japanese dolls made in imitation of western dolls.

DATE
c1900
NATIONALITY
Japanese
AVAILABILITY
easy to find, inexpensive
HEIGHT
7½in (19cm)

69

70 EFFANBEE JOHN WAYNE

Two Effanbee John Wayne dolls. The doll on the left has a bisque head, moulded blue eyes, eyelashes, brows and hair and a cloth body, in cavalry uniform. On the right John Wayne is wearing a cowboy outfit. This doll also has a bisque head and a cloth body.

DATE
c1970
NATIONALITY
American
AVAILABILITY
easy to find, inexpensive
HEIGHT
16in (41cm)

71 COPY OF KAMMER & REINHARDT DOLL

This bisque-headed copy of a Kammer & Reinhardt character doll was made by the Japanese to compete with the German market. She has an open mouth with two teeth, a bent-limbed baby composition body and limbs and open/shut eyes. She is marked "NIPPON, BIO RE", and is a very attractive doll in its frilled and tucked baby dress and bonnet.

DATE
1915
NATIONALITY
Japanese
AVAILABILITY
easy to find, mid-price range
HEIGHT
20in (51cm)

71

72 QUEUE SAN BABY AND CHIN CHIN

Two all-bisque dolls of the same design. The one in the purple and pink bonnet is labelled Queue San Baby and was produced by the Morimura Brothers after the design of Hikozo Araki in 1915. Morimura imported its goods from Japan.

The other doll, of the same design, is labelled Chin Chin and was made by Gebrüder Heubach of Germany. These dolls had various types of moulded headwear and a moulded queue. Their brown eyes had a black pupil whereas the Queue San Baby had only black pupil-less eyes. The index finger was separated on Chin Chin but not on Queue San.

DATE
1915 and 1920s
NATIONALITY
Japanese and German
AVAILABILITY
easy to find, mid-price range
HEIGHT
4½in (11cm) and 4¼in (10.5cm)

72

73 KAMMER & REINHARDT GIRL

This Kammer & Reinhardt toddler doll number 109 is named Elise. She has intaglio eyes, an open/closed mouth and a jointed composition body. The firm of Kammer & Reinhardt specialized in character dolls and this one is a rare example of a girl character.

DATE
1913
NATIONALITY
German
AVAILABILITY
rare, expensive
HEIGHT
18in (46cm)

74 BISQUE BRU DOLL

A Bru bébé doll representing a small girl rather than a baby. This one has the circle and dot mark on it which denotes its early date. She has composition arms and lower legs and a soft body. Her mouth is open/closed and she has the large brown glass eyes and fine modelling typical of her type. Her dress is not original.

DATE
c1880
NATIONALITY
French
AVAILABILITY
rare, expensive
HEIGHT
20in (51cm)

73

74

75

75 JUMEAU IN STRAW BONNET

A fine Jumeau bébé, with fixed paperweight eyes and an open/closed mouth. This is a very pretty doll, typical of many of the Jumeau bébés which were produced about the end of the 19th century. The firm was founded during the mid-19th century and due to fine workmanship and considerable skill in marketing, it became the leading French manufacturer of dolls.

DATE
c1880
NATIONALITY
French
AVAILABILITY
rare, expensive
HEIGHT
24in (61cm)

New Materials

In spite of their apparent fragility, porcelain dolls have survived in considerable numbers, significantly more than dolls made of cloth, wood, wax and papier mâché, but the manufacturers of the late 19th and early 20th century were not satisfied with porcelain and were constantly looking for something more durable. They tried a great many different substances. Composition was quite successful, though not waterproof, but then celluloid seemed at first to satisfy all their requirements, in that it was lightweight, waterproof, seemingly unbreakable, and could be planed, drilled, polished and moulded.

Celluloid had been invented in England in the mid-19th century, and was improved upon by various firms including the Rheinische Gummi- und Celluloid-Fabrik Co in Germany which was producing dolls' heads made of this new substance as early as 1873. The company's mark was a turtle and the dolls are often known as "Turtle dolls" since the actual name is such a long one. Other German doll-makers followed suit and Armand Marseille, Kestner and others made celluloid versions of their bisque dolls, with the same mould numbers and looking like the originals. Even the Grace Putnam Bye-Lo Baby was made with a celluloid head.

In France, celluloid dolls were made by the SNF (Société Nobel Française) and SIC (Société Industrielle de Celluloid) and Petitcolin, which produced some very good-looking dolls. French fashion dolls with leather bodies have been found with celluloid heads, but they are rare.

In England there were several firms making celluloid dolls (among them the London Cascelloid Company), and as they became cheaper, Japan made thousands of them for export.

The first dolls made from celluloid in America were made in about 1880 by the Celluloid Manufacturing Co., followed by many other firms including the Parsons-Jackson Celluloid Collar Co. and the firm of Horsman, which was advertising celluloid dolls in 1912.

Unfortunately, the early promise of celluloid was not fulfilled. The dolls were easily squashed and once squashed, a celluloid doll's face never recovers its original shape, in spite of efforts at restoration with knitting needles and other implements. The colours faded and worse still, the dolls were inflammable.

Manufacturers also tried making rubber dolls. Again, rubber seemed the ideal substance for a child's plaything, soft, unbreakable, paintable and mouldable but again, the surface paint rubbed off and the rubber decomposed.

Charles Goodyear, an American manufacturer, patented a process for making rubber less brittle and his brother patented a rubber doll's head in 1851. Many other manufacturers tried making rubber dolls. As late as 1940, there was a Magic Skin Baby doll, which had a composition head and a body of thin rubber stuffed with cotton and foam.

Manufacturers also tried making metal dolls. Brass, zinc, copper, tin and aluminium were used for doll's heads, some of which are attractive, though the brass heads are very heavy. The metal had to be painted and the paint has not always lasted well. Brass shoulder-heads marked Minerva, which were made in Germany, can be found in the UK.

In America the Atlas Doll & Toy Co made all-metal dolls and the Giebeler-Falk Doll Corp. made interesting dolls with aluminium heads and wood or composition bodies.

The precise date of the invention of hard plastic is difficult to establish but by 1948 the Ideal Toy Co. of America was producing a well-finished doll with a hard plastic head with composition body and limbs, named Baby Coos. This was followed by Brother Coos in 1951 and another Baby Coos with a hard plastic head and a Magic Skin Baby, which was stuffed with foam rubber and cotton. Good quality, hard plastic, which looks much like celluloid, has worn well, but dolls made of low-grade plastic have often split or cracked at the seams. The Madame Alexander Company of America was making hard plastic dolls into the 1950s, gradually changing to plastic and vinyl and then to all-vinyl.

With the introduction of soft vinyl, manufacturers were able to make dolls with rooted wigs which could be washed, cut and styled. The dolls are also soft, unbreakable, washable and can be coloured in naturalistic shades. The nature of the material enables fine casting to be done, so the dolls have plenty of realistic detail. They can, however, be stained with felt-tip or ballpoint pens.

Mattell was another American company making hard plastic dolls, later changing to vinyl. By 1965 Barbie and Ken, Fashion Queen Barbie and other dolls were all-vinyl. Barbie dolls, the original Teenage Fashion Models were the great phenomenon of 1959 and although Barbie look-alikes have come and gone, she remains queen of them all and is seriously collected and discussed in Barbie fan clubs. Collector interest in these dolls has caused prices to rise considerably, so that a Barbie from the first production run is worth over a thousand times what it cost to buy at the time. This much sought-after early model has holes in her feet lined with copper tubing that fits over the prongs of a black plastic stand, while subsequent dolls had wire stands that hooked under the arms.

The most dramatic changes in this doll have been in her hair. Starting with a pony tail, it changed to a bubble cut, then to straight hair in the 1970s and soft flowing tresses in the 1980s. The Fashion Queen Barbie came with moulded hair and three interchangeable wigs.

The British firm of Pedigree Soft Toys Ltd was the first firm in the UK to manufacture high-quality composition dolls by mass production. In 1938 it was advertising its dolls as "almost unbreakable" and by 1948 was making Beauty Skin dolls, which had soft rubber bodies and hard plastic heads. In 1955, made an all-plastic walking doll and in 1963 Sindy doll, a teenage doll similar to Barbie, which was 12in (30cm) high with free-moving arms and legs and hair which could be combed and styled. Like Barbie, the doll had many different fashion outfits to wear and these were updated every year.

Rosebud Dolls was a company formed by Eric Smith in 1947. His firm had previously made composition dolls but later they were made in plastic. He invented a device for making dolls speak and was successful until 1967, when the firm was taken over by the American Mattell Corporation.

From 1966 to 1986, one of the most popular playdolls was the English-made Sasha. This vinyl doll with a pose-able body was produced in Stockport by the Friedland Doggart group to the designs of a Swiss artist named Sasha Morgenthaler. She had been making dolls for about 30 years and believed that a doll should have a sensitive expression which would lend itself to the mood of the child playing with it. If a child's doll could be a friend, then the child would grow to care for it.

The dolls have little facial modelling because she felt that a minimum indication of facial modelling on a doll was better than the excess of it usually found in commercially made dolls. The only dolls Morgenthaler found acceptable were those by Kathe Kruse and Lotte-Sievers-Hahn, but they were very expensive and she wanted her dolls to be reasonably priced. They also have a carefully neutral expression and the skin tones and clothing of real children of all nationalities. The original Sasha dolls measured 20in (51cm) high and wore a wig of natural hair, while the factory-produced Sasha dolls made in England under the name Trendon are 16in (41cm) high and have rooted hair. However, all the Sasha dolls embody her ideas. Sasha Morgenthaler died in 1975 and her work is preserved in the museum of her name in Zurich, Switzerland.

Caring for plastic and vinyl dolls

Hard plastic dolls can easily be cleaned with detergent and water on a soft cloth but it is best not to soak any doll, as the water may seep into the body, become trapped there and cause mould and foul odours. Vinyl is not biodegrade-able and is impervious to decay and insects but it can be damaged by mould which can stain. Remove any stain with a commercial mould remover, testing a small area before applying it to the entire doll.

Ballpoint pen is a common hazard and this too can be absorbed by vinyl and stain it. Working from the outer edge of the stain towards the centre, wash with a cloth soaked in an alcohol such as methylated spirits. Change the cloth as it becomes stained. Anything left will have penetrated the vinyl surface and you can try to remove this with hydrogen peroxide. Do not use bleach, acetone or ammonia.

Collecting modern dolls

Bearing in mind the amazing increase in value of the Barbie doll, now would seem to be the time to buy the latest in vinyl and plastic dolls of all kinds. They are the heirlooms of the future and they are readily available for everyone to buy.

1 CELLULOID HEAD

Kammer & Reinhardt was among the many German firms to make celluloid dolls. This doll, with a celluloid head and composition body, is impressed with the mark "K&R 406/1" and the turtle mark used by Rheinische Gummi- und Celluloid-Fabrik, which often made heads and celluloid doll parts for other firms, so it is not unusual to find these marks together on one doll.

She has sleeping eyes, an open mouth, swivel head, jointed composition body, original hair and is dressed in a bridesmaid's dress.

Rheinische Gummi- und Celluloid-Fabrik were producing celluloid heads for Kammer & Reinhardt as early as 1902.

DATE
1910
NATIONALITY
German
AVAILABILITY
rare, expensive
HEIGHT
15¾in (40cm)

1

2 SWIVEL NECK DOLL

A French doll with a celluloid head made between 1875 and 1900. The head is attached to a swivel neck. The body and costume are of a later date. Two of the most usual marks found on French celluloid dolls are "SNF" (Société Nobel Française, registered 1939 and 1960) and "SIC" (Société Industrielle du Celluloid). Some celluloid dolls are poorly made, but this one is a handsome creature.

DATE
late 19th century
NATIONALITY
French
AVAILABILITY
easy to find, mid-price range
HEIGHT
not known

3 CELLULOID HEAD DOLL

A Kammer & Reinhardt open mouth, glass-eyed doll with a celluloid head and composition body, wearing her original checked dress.

Celluloid heads are found on all kinds of bodies, and their eyes are either painted or sometimes made of glass. The Rheinische Gummi- und Celluloid-Fabrik made most of the celluloid heads for Kammer & Reinhardt.

DATE
early 20th century
NATIONALITY
German
AVAILABILITY
rare, inexpensive
HEIGHT
not known

3

4 FRENCH CELLULOID DOLL

DATE
c1920
NATIONALITY
French
AVAILABILITY
*easy to find,
mid-price range*
HEIGHT
21in (52.5cm)

A French all-celluloid doll with the "Tête de l'aigle" (eagle head) mark of Petitcolin of Paris. The hands are particularly well-modelled.

This firm registered its trademark of a side view of an eagle's head in 1904 and started to make celluloid doll's heads about 1909, in a material called celoid. The hairstyle of this doll dates her to the 1920s.

5 PETITCOLIN DOLL

An all-celluloid character French doll, with a fixed neck, painted features, bent limbs and open/closed mouth by Petitcolin. It is marked with the sideways view of an eagle's head.

The doll is wearing a cotton, lace-trimmed dress and petticoat, a crocheted bonnet and knitted pants.

DATE
c1920
NATIONALITY
French
AVAILABILITY
*easy to find,
inexpensive*
HEIGHT
7in (18cm)

6

6 FRENCH CELLULOID

A celluloid SNF character doll with moulded bobbed hair, fixed glass eyes with lashes, a celluloid body and limbs, jointed shoulders and hips and a swivel neck.

The initials SNF stand for Société Nobel Française, whose mark is one of those most commonly found on French celluloid dolls of this period. The Société Industrielle de Celluloid merged with other companies and its successor was the SNF, using the name Sicoid. The SNF were used from 1927 although the trademark was not registered until 1939. From then on their trademark was a wyvern, a fabulous winged, two-legged cross between a griffin and a dragon.

DATE
c1927
NATIONALITY
French
AVAILABILITY
rare, inexpensive
HEIGHT
17in (43cm)

The doll is wearing her original red flannel dress covered with a white pinafore decorated with drawings of children playing. Underneath, she has a tucked and lace-trimmed petticoat, nylon (presumably replacement) drawers, white socks and pretty red shoes with rosettes.

7 CRAWLING DOLL

This clockwork celluloid doll moves along at great speed when a key in its stomach is wound up. It has the words "Made in Japan" stamped on its feet. The doll is wearing its original romper suit, with a little collar hiding its swivel neck. The body, arms and legs are made of celluloid and the eyes and mouth are painted.

DATE
1940
NATIONALITY
Japanese
AVAILABILITY
rare, inexpensive
HEIGHT
6in (15cm)

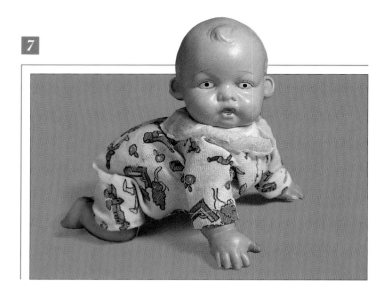

7

8 KESTNER DOLL

This Kestner all-celluloid doll is marked with a "K" that looks like crossed swords. The firm claimed that celluloid dolls were matt-finished and that the colours would not fade in the sun, but as Rheinisches Gummi- und Celluloid-Fabrik supplied most of the major doll-makers with celluloid heads, it is unlikely that there would have been much difference between them. The colours of this bent-limbed character baby have faded somewhat.

DATE
early 20th century
NATIONALITY
German
AVAILABILITY
easy to find, inexpensive
HEIGHT
14in (35.5cm)

8

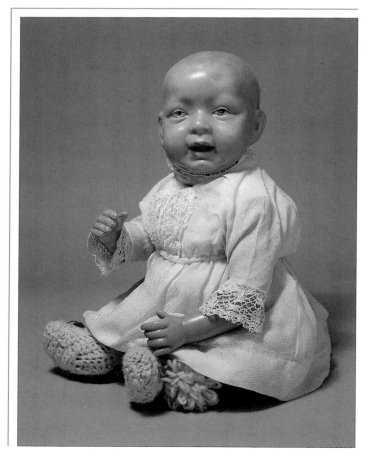

9 CLOCKWORK DOLL

An unusual Japanese mechanical clockwork doll with a celluloid head and metal body housing the clockwork mechanism. She has painted eyes and celluloid limbs and is wearing her original clothes. The word "Japan" is printed on each of the soles of her metal feet.

DATE
c1950
NATIONALITY
Japanese
AVAILABILITY
easy to find, inexpensive
HEIGHT
13½in (34cm)

10 MARKS BROS. DOLL

Marks Bros. of Boston, Massachusetts, USA, made and imported dolls and doll's heads. A number was often placed on the back of their shoulder-heads indicating the height of the head in inches.
This celluloid head has moulded hair and painted features and the number "6" on it.

DATE
1918–30
NATIONALITY
American
AVAILABILITY
rare, inexpensive
HEIGHT
6in (15cm)

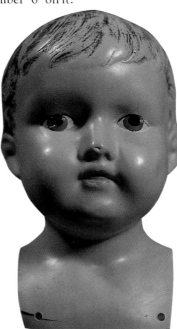

12 CHARACTER DOLL

This character rubber baby doll with an open/closed laughing mouth has not weathered the years very well. Its arms and one foot have completely perished and it is now becoming sticky round the neck, so may not last for much longer. However, it demonstrates the quality of the modelling on this type of doll, and although the colour has faded, it is still an attractive head.

DATE
1920s
NATIONALITY
English
AVAILABILITY
rare, inexpensive
HEIGHT
12½in (32cm)

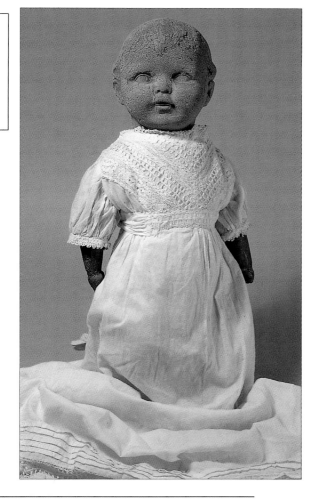

11 JAPANESE SWIMMING DOLL

A Japanese swimming doll with a celluloid head, body and legs, and tin arms, which flail about in the water when the doll is wound up. With her painted eyes and moulded hair, she looks very like the Japanese walking doll on page 104 and could easily have been made by the same firm.

DATE
c1920
NATIONALITY
Japanese
AVAILABILITY
rare, inexpensive
HEIGHT
6in (15cm)

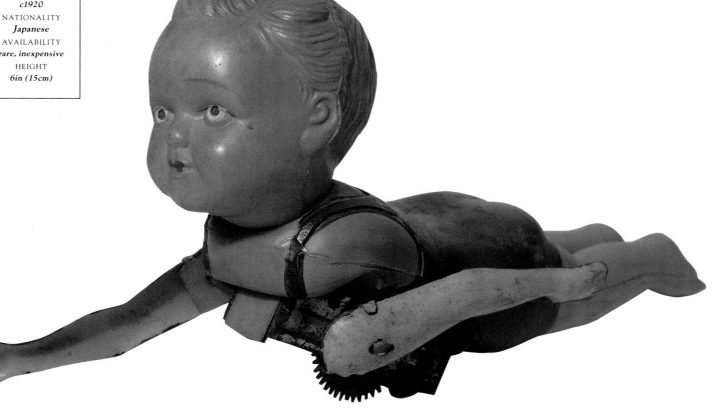

13 GIRL GUIDE

 An amusing little Girl Guide doll with the remains of some of the original paint, which is probably why she is in better condition than the other rubber dolls. The doll had flirty, sideways-looking eyes, the paint of which is still visible. Rubber dolls continued to be made into the 1950s.

DATE
1920s
NATIONALITY
English
AVAILABILITY
rare, inexpensive
HEIGHT
5in (12.5cm)

14 GOODYEAR RUBBER CO. DOLL

The Goodyear Rubber Co. was among several manufacturers that experimented with making rubber dolls. In theory, rubber was an ideal substance for a doll, as it was safe and unbreakable, but unfortunately it has not proved durable.

This Goodyear rubber baby doll of the 1920s, for example, has lost all its paint and some of its skin surface. However, it does give a good idea of the style of the doll, with its rather square, chunky face and chubby neck. The original painted surface would have made it more attractive.

DATE
c1920
NATIONALITY
American
AVAILABILITY
rare, inexpensive
HEIGHT
15in (38cm)

14

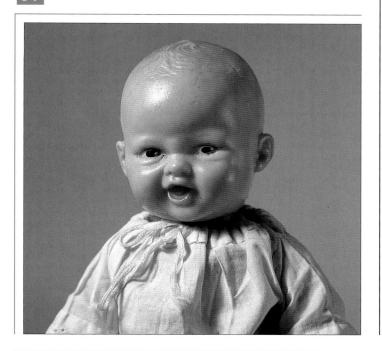

15 NEW YORK RUBBER CO. DOLL

This interesting rubber shoulder-head doll was made by the New York Rubber Co. She has moulded, painted hair and features which are rather worn. The sewn-on footwear and wooden sticks supporting the fingers indicate that the body was made by Philip Goldsmith, who manufactured doll's bodies from 1870 to 1894 in Cincinnati, Ohio. Many types of head, including those from France and Germany, have been found on his bodies. Another feature of this body is that the seat section has a separate piece inserted and the legs placed in the front portion, so that the doll can sit easily.

DATE
1880s
NATIONALITY
American
AVAILABILITY
easy to find, mid-price range
HEIGHT
14in (35.5cm)

16 MINERVA HEAD

Minerva painted brass heads on shoulder-plates like this are the most commonly found in Britain. They were made at the turn of the century by A. Vischer of Germany, which also made heads in tin. Buschow & Beck also used the name Minerva on its metal heads.

The brass heads, which had fixed glass eyes, were coated with a new type of celluloid washable enamel and this has lasted well. The rest of the body would probably have been made of wood.

DATE
early 20th century
NATIONALITY
German
AVAILABILITY
rare, inexpensive
HEIGHT
4in (10cm)

16

17 ACTION MAN

Two metal dolls with composition heads, hands and feet. The rest of the body is made of metal parts, which have been rolled, shaped and pressed. The balls at the joints are hollow, and the joints come apart so that the dolls can be placed in any position.
One of the dolls is dressed in its original Edwardian dress. On both dolls is the name Serba of Switzerland. They are really early Action Men.

DATE
c1921
NATIONALITY
Swiss
AVAILABILITY
rare, inexpensive
HEIGHT
7½in (19cm)

17

18 ALUMINIUM HEAD DOLL

The Giebeler-Falk Corp. (1918–21) made dolls with aluminium heads, hands and feet. The rest of the body was composition and wood. This doll has a wig, metal sleeping eyes and an open/closed mouth with four teeth. She is jointed, even at the wrists and ankles. The doll has the number 22 in her mark because she is 22in tall.

DATE
c1919
NATIONALITY
American
AVAILABILITY
rare, expensive
HEIGHT
22in (56cm)

18

19 HARD PLASTIC DOLL

The British National Doll Co. was making dolls with china heads in 1933. In 1942 the firm claimed to be the first to mass-produce composition dolls and by 1950 it was making hard plastic dolls like this one, marked "BND London" and is wearing its original romper suit.
It has open/shut eyes, an open/closed mouth, bent limbs and moulded hair. It is jointed at hips, shoulder and wrists and has a swivel neck.
The mould lines can be seen clearly down the sides of the legs.

DATE
1950
NATIONALITY
English
AVAILABILITY
rare, inexpensive
HEIGHT
10in (25cm)

19

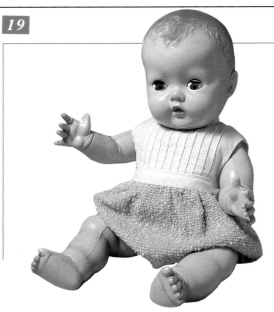

20 MADAME ALEXANDER DOLLS

The Madame Alexander Doll Co. of America was founded by Madame Alexander in 1923. She came from a family which had been connected with dolls for generations. Early dolls produced by the company were made of cloth, but it has made dolls in nearly every new material in the 60 plus years since then. The company changed hands in 1988 and Madame Alexander died in 1990.

The blond doll here has her head incised "3 Alexander 1979" and is known as Little Brother. There is also a Little Sister, not shown here.

The dark-haired model is known as Baby Precious and she is dated 1974. The dolls have vinyl limbs, stuffed soft bodies, rooted hair and open/closed eyes. They are wearing their original clothes.

DATE
1970s
NATIONALITY
American
AVAILABILITY
easy to find, inexpensive
HEIGHT
15in (38cm)

21 BEJUSA DOLLS

Two uncannily realistic vinyl dolls made in the 1980s by the Spanish firm Bejusa. The large doll is an open-mouthed toddler walking doll, operated by batteries. It has moulded hair, two teeth, open/closed eyes and a soft toddler body, not jointed at knees or elbows. The neck is fixed.

It is wearing its original clothes of romper suit, cardigan and boots.

The new-born baby has half-open eyes, a swivel neck and perfectly modelled hands, feet and genitals. It has an all-vinyl body and bent arms and legs jointed at hips and shoulders. It is wearing a romper suit, nappy, vest, knitted jacket and leggings. It arrived in its own carry cot with its own identification certificate.

DATE
1980s
NATIONALITY
Spanish
AVAILABILITY
easy to find, mid-price range
HEIGHT
25in (63.5cm)
20in (51cm)

21

22 PEDIGREE ENGLISH DOLLS

The larger Pedigree doll has flirty, open/shut eyes, moulded curly hair, a swivel head, bent arms that move from the shoulders and slightly bent legs that move from the hips. She is a talking doll, with a voice box at the back. The smaller doll is similar, but rather more faded.

This model head was also made to fit the rubber Beauty Skin doll, which was stuffed with kapok.

DATE
1948–1950s
NATIONALITY
English
AVAILABILITY
rare, inexpensive
HEIGHT
24in (61cm)
13in (33cm)

22

23 VINYL KEWPIE

The Kewpie doll, originally designed by Rose O'Neill about 1913, has kept its popularity right until the present day, as this little vinyl doll shows. It has the same topknot of hair, sideways glance and "starfish" hands seen on the bisque versions.

This doll has a swivel neck and is jointed at the shoulders and hip.

DATE
1970s
NATIONALITY
English
AVAILABILITY
easy to find, inexpensive
HEIGHT
9in (23cm)

24 CABBAGE PATCH KIDS

A phenomenon of the 1980s, the Cabbage Patch dolls had record-breaking sales for some time and were made in all sizes.

These tiny versions of the dolls (marked "OAA") were made in China in 1984. They are extremely well-made, with jointed shoulders and hips, swivel heads and a good finish in the bright colours loved by children.

DATE
1984
NATIONALITY
Chinese
AVAILABILITY
easy to find, inexpensive
HEIGHT
4in (10cm)

24

25 SUPERMAN AND ACTION MAN

Superman (left) was made by the MEGO Corp of Hong Kong in about 1977. He has a swivel head and waist, jointed shoulders, elbows, wrists and knees. He has "D. C. Comics Inc." written on his neck and his fine manly torso is encased in a blue and red nylon romper suit, topped by a red nylon cloak. His red plastic boots are a snug fit.

Action Man, made in England by Palitoy under license from Hasbro in 1964, is full of amazing detail in plastic. Hung about with a gun, grenades, a knife in a holster, cartridge holders, binoculars and water bottle, he is ready for action with "AFRIKAKORPS", the name written on his armband. He even has a scar on his face. His short stubby hair is hidden under his cap. He has jointed hips, knees, elbows, shoulders, wrists and ankles. Hasbro also made a GI Joe doll.

Palitoy was taken over by General Mills of America in 1968.

DATE
1964, 1977
NATIONALITY
Hong Kong and English
AVAILABILITY
easy to find, inexpensive
HEIGHT
12in (30.5cm)
13in (33cm)

25

26 "NEGRO" DOLL

A "negro" baby doll with bent limbs, made in hard plastic and typical of many such made in the 1950s. It has curly moulded hair and open/closed eyes, a swivel head and jointed shoulders and hips.

DATE
1952
NATIONALITY
probably English
AVAILABILITY
rare, inexpensive
HEIGHT
15in (38cm)

27 CINDERELLA

A plastic Cinderella doll with open/closed eyes, wearing her original blond wig. She has a swivel neck and is jointed at the shoulders and hips. "Cinderella" is written on the soles of her shoes, which are removable. This is a well-cast doll but not very well finished, as there are moulding ridges down the sides of her arms, legs and head.

DATE
c1950
NATIONALITY
English
AVAILABILITY
rare, inexpensive
HEIGHT
8in (20cm)

28 QUEEN ELIZABETH II

Peggy Nisbet started making dolls in 1953, when she designed a 7in (18cm) model of Queen Elizabeth II to commemorate her coronation. The doll was made of fine bisque and was dressed in coronation robes. Only 250 models were made, and these were sold by the London department store, Harrods.

Peggy Nisbet went on to make over 600 other historical and national costume dolls, using plastics. Among them was this 7in (18cm) high replica of the first Nisbet doll.

Jack Wilson became chairman and managing director in 1975, and in 1989 the House of Nisbet joined forces with R. Dakin Company of San Francisco.

DATE
1970s
NATIONALITY
English
AVAILABILITY
easy to find, inexpensive
HEIGHT
7in (18cm)

28

29

29 NISBET HISTORICAL FIGURES

A group of early Nisbet dolls including Queen Margaret of Scotland, Queen Eleanor of Aquitaine, Henry II and Queen Berengaria.

The complete collection of Nisbet dolls is on loan to a local museum, where it has a room set aside for it.

DATE
1960s
NATIONALITY
English
AVAILABILITY
easy to find, inexpensive
HEIGHT
7in (18cm)

30 ZEEPVAT HISTORICAL FIGURES

 This charming model in air-hardening clay of Kaiser Wilhelm II and his son Prince Wilhelm was made by the English doll artist, Charlotte Zeepvat.
A master's degree in history and historical research combined with her amazing natural artistic skill enable Charlotte Zeepvat to specialize in making her miniature models from photographs. Victorian royalty is one of her favourite subjects. One of her models, a portrait group of Queen Mary with her second son, later George VI, is on display at Windsor Castle.

DATE
1970s
NATIONALITY
English
AVAILABILITY
*easy to find,
mid-price range*
HEIGHT
8in (20cm)

30

31 | SASHA DOLLS

DATE
c1970
NATIONALITY
Swiss
AVAILABILITY
*easy to find,
mid-price range*
HEIGHT
16in (41cm)

In 1965 John and Sara Doggart of Stockport, England, began making dolls designed by a Swiss artist named Sasha Morgenthaler, a successful partnership that lasted until 1986. Morgenthaler had been making dolls for about 30 years, and believed that a doll should have a sensitive expression, which would lend itself to the mood of a child, that it should have little facial modelling and that it should be dressed like a real child. The vinyl Sasha dolls made in England under the name Trendon embodied her ideas. Sasha Morgenthaler died in 1975, and there is a museum of her work in Zurich.

32 GENERAL MILLS DOLLS

A vinyl-headed doll with a hard plastic body made by General Mills, USA. It has open/closed eyes, an open/closed smiling mouth, jointed hips and shoulders and a swivel neck.

It also has swivel wrists and a jointed waist, so that when the battery-operated mechanism is activated by a string, the doll bows and turns from the waist.

DATE
1970
NATIONALITY
American
AVAILABILITY
*easy to find,
inexpensive*
HEIGHT
19in (48cm)

33 HASBRO AND AMERICAN DOLL & TOY CO.

In 1959 Mattel launched its Barbie doll, which was rapturously received by the teenage world. Barbie was essentially a fashion doll, and she was followed by many others of the same type.

It is interesting to see how the dolls have changed from 1963, the date of Tressy by the American Doll & Toy Co. Tressy is wearing a simple cotton dress and the only startling thing about her is the fact that her hair "grows" when a key in her back is turned. The other doll, by Hasbro, wearing a Sindy dress, is dated 1988 and is an altogether more sophisticated model.

DATE
1963 and 1988
NATIONALITY
American
AVAILABILITY
*easy to find,
inexpensive*
HEIGHT
12in (30cm)

33

Cloth Dolls

Cloth dolls have always been objects of love and affection for children, and rag dolls have been found in the ancient tombs of Egypt and Peru, where the dry climate has preserved them. However, because cloth is so easily damaged by dirt, damp and other environmental hazards, most rag dolls have not lasted well, and it is only those from the last century that provide us with any examples to examine.

The French, such skilled makers of bisque dolls, had little to show in the way of cloth dolls until the 1920s, when they produced some very fine boudoir dolls. Their modern doll-artists are now making very lovely fabric dolls, but strangely enough it was Italy, a country with little tradition of doll-making, that has produced the world's most famous cloth dolls.

Lenci is the trademark and name of the firm making felt dolls with felt-pressed faces which was founded by Elena Konig, who married Enrico Scavini in 1915. While Enrico went to fight in the war, Elena and her brother made dolls in their apartment in Turin. Their first doll, dressed in a red and white felt dress, was called Lencina. After the war, the firm grew and in 1922 it registered its trademark. Elena continued to design dolls herself for some time but well-known artists were later commissioned to expand the range and the firm continues in production to this day.

The variety and charm of the Lenci dolls, with their felt heads and bodies and beautiful felt clothes, make them desirable to collectors and there is a wide variety to choose from – costume dolls, ethnic dolls, film star and historical dolls, as well as children. They are instantly recognizable by their sideways glancing eyes and sometimes sulky expression. Some have real hair, some have mohair, and they are marked in various ways – the earliest mark was a metal tag. Because of their popularity, there have been many similar felt dolls of this type during this century.

A complete contrast of style is provided by the cloth dolls of a German artist, Kathe Kruse. Her numerous children were models for her dolls, which she made initially to amuse them. Her first attempt at making a doll was a knotted kitchen towel filled with sand for a body and a potato for a head, which was a great success with her small daughter. Kathe Kruse soon became obsessed with doll-making. In 1910 she exhibited an improved model at a department store in Berlin and this launched her on her career.

Another German maker of cloth dolls, in quite a different style, was Margarete Steiff, of the Steiff toy-making family. Margarete Steiff made felt-headed dolls as early as 1894, most of them with a seam that runs down the centre of the face, giving them a rather frightening appearance. However, she was trying to get away from the sickly sweet dolls that were produced by most factories and in this she succeeded. The dolls were made to stand by being given large, flat feet.

Although English porcelain dolls had never been of the first quality, in the early years of the 20th century there were a great many first-rate English makers of fabric dolls. Chad Valley was founded in 1823, moving to Wellington, Shropshire, in 1915, and specializing in promotional toys, which were well-known characters in newspapers, books or cartoon films. One of the first was Bonzo, the bull terrier puppy invented by the artist Studdy for the *Daily Sketch*. There were the Mabel Lucie Atwell dolls in the 1920s, models of Princess Elizabeth and her sister Margaret Rose in the 1930s, boudoir night-dress cases and Snow White and the Seven Dwarfs, all of which were very popular.

Perhaps the most prolific of the English fabric doll-makers was Dean's Rag Book Co. Ltd, a subsidiary of Dean & Son Ltd, which was founded in 1905 to print rag books and rag dolls. The company patented a great many inventions, among them one for "dolls, puppets, figures, toy animals etc of inflatable and uninflatable portions enclosed within a fabric or other cover shaped to the outline of the complete article". Its cut-out cloth dolls, called Knockabout had various subjects, the most popular of which was Big Baby Doll, with separate clothes provided for them.

For many years there was no indigenous doll-making industry in America and dolls were imported from Europe but among the early American cloth doll-makers was Izannah Walker, who made dolls of stiffened stockinette with oil-painted features and hair. She patented her dolls in 1873 but it is thought that she actually began producing them well before that date. Izannah Walker dolls are rare and not to be found outside America.

Martha Chase dolls are another prized collectors' doll. A face with raised features was covered in stockinette, sized and hardened, then painted in oil colours like those of Izannah Walker. Her dolls were at first made for family and friends but they became so popular that she started a small factory at Pawtucket, Rhode Island, to produce them commercially.

Introduced in America in 1810, rotary printing presses enabled textiles to be patterned quickly and economically, and this invention gave manufacturers the idea of making printed cloth dolls. The retailer simply had to sell the cloth by the yard and the rest of the work could be done at home. Edward Peck was the first to be granted a patent for his printed Santa Claus, which is now a rare collector's item. He was followed by the Arnold Print Works of North Adams, Massachusetts, which by 1892 had produced a tabby cat, and then a line of animals and dolls depicting popular characters of the day. It also printed soldiers, nursery stories and black dolls.

The other large manufacturer of printed cloth dolls was Art Fabric Mills of New York, Connecticut and London, which sold its. goods by mail order. The dolls included Punch and Judy, Buster Brown and the Life-Size Doll, patented in 1900.

There were other producers of dolls-by-the-yard, including the Cocheco Co., the Saalfield Co., which printed a Kate Greenaway doll and a Little Red Riding Hood, and of course the Kellogs Co., which made its famous Goldilocks and the Three Bears. Advertisers were not slow to realize the potential of promoting their wares through dolls and other give-aways.

Caring for cloth dolls

Cloth dolls can arrive in a sorry state, torn, greasy and with unidentified stains on them. It is difficult to clean rag dolls, for much as one would like to plunge them into hot, soapy water, they would not benefit from such rough treatment.

One method of cleaning, recommended by the owner of the Lilliput Museum, Isle of Wight, UK, is to put some borax in a bag with the doll and shake it. Remove the doll and give it a gentle brushing. You could also sprinkle the doll with fuller's earth and brush that off. There are also spray-on cleaners used for removing fabric and furniture stains, but it would be advisable to try a small inconspicuous area before embarking on a whole-scale cleaning with any chemical.

The doll may have been attacked by moths, in which case use spray-on moth-proofers. A little neat stitching of moth holes and torn limbs and replacement of leaking stuffing, can only do good.

Collecting cloth dolls

Some cloth dolls are well within the range of the modest collector, though early American and German cloth dolls are expensive. It might be better to concentrate on collecting printed cloth toys and advertising dolls, many of which are obainable today.

1 PERUVIAN CLOTH DOLL

 All cloth dolls suffer from the ravages of time, which means that early examples are extremely rare. That there were cloth dolls even in the earliest days of civilization is proved by those found preserved in the dry tombs of Egypt and Peru.

This child's play doll in woven textile from Peru dates from the 1st century, and it was recovered from a child's tomb. Similar Peruvian woven textile dolls can be seen in museums and private collections in different parts of the world.

DATE
1st century
NATIONALITY
Peruvian
AVAILABILITY
rare, expensive
HEIGHT
approx 12in (30.5cm)

2 ART FABRIC MILLS DOLL

 The Art Fabric Mills of New York produced several cloth dolls in the 1900s, among them a life-sized doll in heavy material with gusseted feet, enabling it to stand.

This doll still has the remains of her printed hair and hair ribbon. She has a stuffed body with basic stumps for hands, printed red stockings and black printed boots with laces. On the sole of one boot is written "Art Fabric Mills, New York".

DATE
c1900
NATIONALITY
American
AVAILABILITY
easy to find, inexpensive
HEIGHT
25in (62.5cm)

3 MARTHA CHASE DOLL

 Martha Chase of Pawtucket, Rhode Island, USA, began making dolls just for her family and friends, but they were so successful that they were soon produced commercially. By 1922 19 different models were being made. She died in 1925 but the firm was carried on by her husband and son for many years.

The doll's heads were made with stockinet stretched over a mask. The fabric was then sized and painted with oil paints. This painted cloth doll has rigid arms and cloth legs, hinged at the knee. She is unmarked and has been overpainted at a later date.

DATE
early 20th century
NATIONALITY
American
AVAILABILITY
easy to find, mid-price range
HEIGHT
20in (45cm)

2

3

4 SUNNY JIM

 Sunny Jim was a cloth advertising doll for Force (malted toasted wheat flakes), which was introduced into the UK from the USA.

Original characters were Jim Dumps, who had personality problems because he didn't breakfast on Force and Sunny Jim, a happy person because he did. Jim Dumps was discontinued after a while.

The first Sunny Jim doll was made in the 1920s, when he could be obtained for a certain number of cereal packet tops. Production ceased during World War II but started again in 1955. The doll never sold in the United States.

DATE
1920s
NATIONALITY
English
AVAILABILITY
easy to find, inexpensive
HEIGHT
16in (41cm)

5 KATHE KRUSE DOLL

 Kathe Kruse was a German artist, married to a sculptor, who used her own children as models for her cloth dolls, which she originally made for them. The doll's heads were made of painted, stiffened muslin, moulded in two halves, which were joined together and filled with stuffing. The bodies were made of layers of cotton wound round an armature.

These two Kathe Kruse dolls are typical of her work. They have painted, realistic-looking faces; the boy has painted hair, as was usual from 1910 to 1929, and the girl has a wig, so is probably a later model. She is signed and numbered on the left foot. The cloth hands have suggestions of fingers.

DATE
1920–30
NATIONALITY
German
AVAILABILITY
easy to find, mid-price price
HEIGHT
17in (43cm)
approx 21in (53cm)

6 KATHE KRUSE DOLL II

 This doll looks very much like the boy doll on the left. She has the same painted hair and solemn expression, and she looks very attractive in her Dutch national dress, complete with cap and clogs.

All Kathe Kruse dolls have closed mouths. The fingers are together, the thumb is an extra digit, sewn on. The body is jointed at shoulders and hips. The dolls were advertised as being "Lifelike reproductions, soft, durable, washable, made entirely by hand of impregnated nettle-cloth".

DATE
c1925
NATIONALITY
German
AVAILABILITY
easy to find, mid-price range
HEIGHT
17in (43cm)

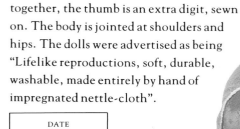

7 KATHE KRUSE BABY

Kathe Kruse developed a baby doll in 1925 to help teach baby care to young mothers. Weighted with sand, it weighed about 5½lb (2.5kg) and was 20in (50cm) long, the height and weight of a new-born baby. The first doll, with closed eyes, was called Traumerchen, the second version with open eyes and unweighted, introduced later in 1925, was known as Du Mein. There were numerous variations on both models. The doll with closed eyes is quite rare.

DATE	*c1925*
NATIONALITY	*German*
AVAILABILITY	*rare, expensive*
HEIGHT	*20in (50cm)*

8 TENNIS PLAYER

Lenci is the name of the firm famous for its felt dolls with pressed felt faces, which it has been making since about 1918, when Elena, the wife of Enrico Scavini, and her brother made their first dolls in the family apartment in Turin.

Early in 1919 the firm was founded officially, with dolls designed at first by Elena, then later by artists.

Liberty of London sold Lenci dolls and this one was bought there in 1925. Called the Tennis Player, he has the brown sideways-glancing eyes typical of Lenci dolls and she is wearing her original clothes and shoes. She has the number 5 on the sole of one foot, which makes the doll something of a rarity.

DATE	*1925*
NATIONALITY	*Italian*
AVAILABILITY	*rare, expensive*
HEIGHT	*18in (46cm)*

9 LENCI DOLL

This Lenci doll has curly hair sewn on in strips and painted, sideways-glancing eyes. Her mouth is closed and she has a stuffed felt body.

Early Lenci dolls were mainly ethnic, character and little girl dolls and they were all designed by Elena Scavini. As the firm grew larger, well-known artists designed the wide variety of dolls which can be found today. The firm still exists, making fine quality felt dolls.

DATE	*c1920*
NATIONALITY	*Italian*
AVAILABILITY	*easy to find, mid-price price*
HEIGHT	*approx 12in (30cm)*

10 CHAD VALLEY DOLL

Chad Valley Dolls of Birmingham, UK, was founded in 1823. It specialized in promotional toys and in film cartoon or book or comic strip characters. One of the first was Bonzo, a bull terrier pup immortalized by the *Daily Sketch* newspaper.

This HMS *Furious* sailor doll was designed about 1935 by Norah Wellings, who worked for Chad Valley for seven years. These sailor dolls were sold as souvenirs on ocean-going liners. When Norah Wellings left Chad Valley she made her own versions of the sailor doll and these, too, were sold on board ship.

DATE
c1935
NATIONALITY
English
AVAILABILITY
easy to find, inexpensive
HEIGHT
approx 10½in (27cm)

11 GEORGE

A Chad Valley doll based on a cartoon figure by Tom Webster which appeared in the *Daily Mirror* newspaper. He and his clothes are made of felt.

Soft toys were very popular in the 1930s, and Chad Valley was most successful with strip cartoon characters like this and with others such as Felix the cat and Pip, Squeak and Wilfred.

DATE
c1930
NATIONALITY
English
AVAILABILITY
easy to find, inexpensive
HEIGHT
11in (28cm)

12 DEAN'S RAG BOOK DOLL

A fine example of a large Dean's Rag Book doll. The company was founded in London in 1903 and in the following years it made rag books and cloth cut-out dolls, among others. By the 1920s, it was improving its cloth dolls, and the Tru-to-life series was launched, with moulded features.

Character dolls, personalities, Lenci-type dolls, velvet-faced dolls, dancing dolls, Mickey Mouse dolls, advertising dolls and dozens of others poured from the Dean's Rag Book factory, yet few have survived, due to the fragile nature of their material.

DATE
c1930
NATIONALITY
English
AVAILABILITY
easy to find, mid-price range
HEIGHT
39in (1m)

13 DEAN'S RAG BOOK DOLL II

A Dean's large fashion doll, dressed in a modern purple satin trouser suit and smart shoes. Her hair is mohair, and she is more like a boudoir doll than the usual Deans' "little girl" dolls. She has a mask face of moulded stockinet and painted features.

Dean's Rag Book Company produced dozens of different dolls, as well as some charming mascot characters such as Dismal Desmond, the spotted dog (found in standing, sitting, cheerful and morose forms), Bunnikins and Sam.

DATE
c1930
NATIONALITY
English
AVAILABILITY
easy to find, mid-price price
HEIGHT
42in (107cm)

14 J. K. FARNELL GEORGE VI DOLL

The firm of J. K. Farnell was founded in about 1871 by Miss Farnell, and made velvet and cloth mascots and animals. In the 1920s it produced dolls with felt faces and many other soft toys. One of its famous character dolls was Ole Bill, a World War I cartoon soldier.

In 1937 it made a set of dolls representing King George VI in Grenadier Guards, Air Force and Scots Guard uniform (seen here). It had also prepared a set of coronation dolls representing the Duke of Windsor as Edward VIII.

DATE	*1937*
NATIONALITY	*English*
AVAILABILITY	*easy to find, inexpensive*
HEIGHT	*15½in (39cm)*

15 CLOTH DOLLS

On the left is a portrait of Dame Anna Neagle as Peter Pan by J. K. Farnell. When Dame Anna visited Mrs Burrows, the former owner of the firm, she told her that the doll was probably sold in the foyer of the theatre in 1938, when she played Peter Pan. In the centre is a Chad Valley doll by Mabel Lucie Atwell. The smaller Lenci doll is dressed in the grey shorts and black shirt of the Fascist movement. Behind him is another Lenci, and on the left is Tich, a cartoon character from the *Daily Mirror* and the *Sunday Pictorial*, made in 1932 by Cartoon Novelties, New Oxford Street, London.

DATE	*1920s and 1930s*
NATIONALITY	*English and Italian*
AVAILABILITY	*easy to find, inexpensive*
HEIGHT	*18½in (47cm) to 10in (25cm)*

16 NORAH WELLINGS DOLLS

DATE	*1926–1960*
NATIONALITY	*English*
AVAILABILITY	*easy to find, inexpensive*
HEIGHT	*14in (37cm)*

These two cloth dolls by Norah Wellings, with felt faces and velvet uniforms, represent members of the WRAF and the WRNS. During World War II Norah Wellings was made Doll-maker to the British Commonwealth of Nations and as a consequence, she designed many dolls representing members of the various armed forces. One favourite was a parachutist named Harry the Hawk, a percentage of whose sales went to the RAF Comforts Fund.

Norah Wellings started her career at Chad Valley, leaving in the mid-1920s to start her own factory with her brother, Leonard. An early commission was to make mascot sailor dolls for sale on the Cunard liners. As they were firmly marked on the sole of the foot with a stitched label, her fame soon spread. The sailors were produced until 1960, when the Wellings factory closed, but Peggy Nisbet (see page 111) continued making them for some time.

Norah Wellings designed dozens of different dolls of different nationalities and sizes.

17 NORAH WELLINGS DOLL II

A very beautiful large felt doll by Norah Wellings, with pressed felt face, painted features and jointed felt body. The fingers are all separate, the wig is mohair, the smiling mouth is closed and the eyes painted. She is wearing her original 1930s dress.

Wellings' dolls were created in a variety of sizes from 7½in (18cm) to as large as 38in (90cm). They all have swivel heads, some are fully jointed, others not. All were originally labelled. This one is called Lucy.

DATE
1930s
NATIONALITY
English
AVAILABILITY
easy to find, inexpensive
HEIGHT
31½in (80cm)

17

18 PRINCE WILLIAM

By the time she was six years old, doll artist Vina Cooke was making her own versions of Snow White and the Seven Dwarfs, and after she married and had a child she turned her hand to making dolls for her out of stockinet. People liked her dolls so she continued to make them, perfecting her technique and discovering that she had a flair for portraits.

This portrait of Prince William as a child is typical of her work, which she considers to be cloth sculpture. She does not make a mask for her cloth dolls; she uses cloth, wire, stuffing and a little glue, and she paints the faces. Her dolls are found in many collections.

DATE
1983
NATIONALITY
English
AVAILABILITY
easy to find, inexpensive
HEIGHT
approx 20in (51cm)

19 BOUDOIR DOLL

Boudoir dolls were designed for adults and were fashionable in the 1920s. They were usually in the form of heavily made-up, leggy women with elegant clothes and coiffeurs.

They were made in England by many firms including Dean's. The French versions are attactive, usually painted on silk stockinet or pressed fabric, with eyelashes and heavily accentuated eyes. The dolls are always long and slim and have a slight air of depravity about them, which makes them totally unsuitable as playthings – which they are not.

This one is rather more ladylike than most. She has a painted stockinet face with big eyes, a cloth body and limbs jointed at knee and elbow. She has a tiny waist and large bust. All her clothes are original: underwear, satin dress, diamanté-and-lace trims, hat with floral organza decoration and flowers, and high-heeled shoes.

DATE
1920s
NATIONALITY
probably French
AVAILABILITY
easy to find, inexpensive
HEIGHT
41in (102.5cm)

19

20 CLOTH BOUDOIR DOLL

This cloth boudoir doll with a pressed fabric head and composition hands and legs has stranded silk hair, large painted eyes with huge eyelashes and is dressed in 1930s style.

Boudoir dolls were also the fashion in America, where they were inspired by the movie idols. Portrait dolls of celebrities such as Lillian Gish, Gloria Swanson and others were photographed with the stars for publicity shots.

DATE
1920–30
NATIONALITY
probably French
AVAILABILITY
*easy to find,
inexpensive*
HEIGHT
30in (76cm)

21 ETHNIC PLAY DOLLS

A distinctive group of Helene McLeod's stuffed cloth playdolls. They all have hard-wearing latex heads covered with stockinette. Their features are painted and all the clothing is removable and washable.

Helene McLeod, a member of the British Dollmaker's Association, is well known for her African and Asian figures, although she does also make dolls of European appearance. She has spent almost two decades in various parts of Africa, including Nigeria, Mauritius, Lesotho, Botswana and Swaziland, and her dolls have all been lovingly observed from real life.

DATE
1980s
NATIONALITY
British
AVAILABILITY
easy to find, inexpensive
HEIGHT
14–16in (35.5–41cm)

21

22 STEIFF GIRL

The German firm of Steiff is best known for its long line of teddy bears, but it also made dolls, designed by Margarete Steiff, from 1894. Her dolls are instantly recognizable by the seam running down the centre of the face. The dolls, which have felt masks and button eyes, are not pretty, as can be seen from this picture, but Margarete Steiff did not intend them to be so. She was trying to get away from the stereotype "little girl" doll and she succeeded.

The dolls are sturdily made and are able to stand on their own feet. This one has plaited wool hair and an open mouth.

DATE
c1910
NATIONALITY
German
AVAILABILITY
rare, expensive
HEIGHT
15in (38cm)

22

23 STEIFF BOY

This Steiff boy has the same central seam on his face, which, with his wispy hair and little button eyes, gives him a rather strange appearance. Steiff dolls were not made in very large sizes but this one, at 23in (58.5cm), is a large one.

Margarete Steiff died in 1909 and was succeeded by her two nephews. Many of the Steiff dolls were designed by the artist Albert Schlopsnies.

DATE
c1910
NATIONALITY
German
AVAILABILITY
rare, expensive
HEIGHT
23in (58.5cm)

23

24 DEAN'S TRU-TO-LIFE DOLL

The Tru-to-life series of dolls by Dean's could be bought in sheet form or ready-made from the factory, where they were pressed on to a stiff backing to produce a moulded face. This technique for making more realistic-looking rag dolls was patented in 1913, and the doll shown here demonstrates it.

There were a great many different designs for the Tru-to-life cloth dolls, both dressed and undressed, when they wore this attractive lace-trimmed chemise and pants outfit. Another innovation in the Tru-to-life series was the fact that the dolls' feet had soles to enable them to stand. These are clearly seen here, with the Dean's mark on them.

> DATE
> *c1913*
> NATIONALITY
> *English*
> AVAILABILITY
> *easy to find,
> inexpensive*
> HEIGHT
> *13in (33cm)*

25 BOOKIE'S RUNNER

This amusing doll, probably designed as a mascot for the racing fraternity, is a Bookie's Runner. Though this doll is not marked, it is thought to be by Dean's Rag Book Co. Ltd, which made a great many character dolls and mascots including a Modern Beau Brummel, Popeye and Henry, based on a popular cartoon. This doll, with his loud checked coat, pipe, money bag and red face, could be one of the line.

> DATE
> *c1930*
> NATIONALITY
> *English*
> AVAILABILITY
> *easy to find,
> mid-price range*
> HEIGHT
> *13in (33cm)*

24

26 RUSSIAN TEA COSY DOLL

An early 20th-century Russian "tea cosy" doll on a quilted base, designed to keep a small samovar warm. The face and hands are made of felt.

This type of doll appears to be a traditional one in Russia. The doll was bought at Moscow Airport in 1952 and there are similar dolls in other museums. One version dated about 1925, is called The Gossip and the head is made of moulded stockinet. Later versions have plastic heads and hands.

> DATE
> *early 20th century*
> NATIONALITY
> *Russia*
> AVAILABILITY
> *rare, expensive*
> HEIGHT
> *17in (43cm)*

26

27 MISSION DOLLS

Made for sale in Hong Kong by the Christian Family Service Centre, Kwun Tong, these two little dolls are handmade, with pale pink silk heads and bodies and black wool hair. Their faces are embroidered in silk and they are wearing nicely made silk tunics and trousers.

DATE
20th century
NATIONALITY
Chinese
AVAILABILITY
rare, inexpensive
HEIGHT
8in (20cm)
6½in (16.5cm)

28 BROWNIE

Although not very finely made, this doll by an unknown maker is unmistakably a Brownie and it is also a factory-made doll. The uniform has been given quite a lot of attention – the belt, for example, could not have been made at home. The Brownie badges are quite basic, the face is painted and the hair is suggested by two clumps of wool. The feet do not stand as firmly as those of most Dean's dolls.

DATE
1974
NATIONALITY
English
AVAILABILITY
rare, inexpensive
HEIGHT
15in (38cm)

27

29 BOUDOIR DOLLS

Two pairs of identical boudoir ladies, made of cloth with pressed canvas faces, dressed in their original clothes. One is labelled "Poupées Gerb's, 29 Rue Gouthey, Paris. Made in France".
These dolls are four of several that were luckily rescued in the nick of time from potential destruction on a bonfire.

DATE
c1920
NATIONALITY
French
AVAILABILITY
rare, mid-price range
HEIGHT
29in (74cm)

29

30 UNCUT CUT-OUT CLOTH DOLL

Celia and Charity Smith were among the many designers who explored the potential of new printing techniques on fabric. Their first doll, which had hair and features printed on it, was made in two pieces with the instruction to "Sew together and stuff with cotton batting and sawdust".

Charity Smith sold her patent to the Arnold Print Works in 1892, but the doll shown here was manufactured by Cocheco in 1889. The dolls were sold by the yard in drapers' shops and general stores.

DATE
1889
NATIONALITY
American
AVAILABILITY
*easy to find,
inexpensive*
HEIGHT
15½in (39.5cm)

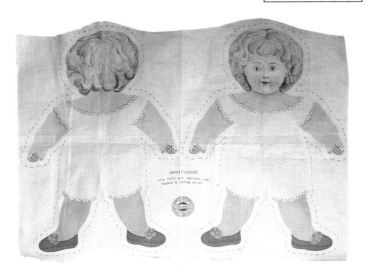

31 BALSAM BABY

Balsam Baby was the US trademark name for a cloth doll made by Gre-Poir. She has a moulded cloth mask face with painted features, a partial wig and the body is jointed at neck, shoulders and hips. The fingers are indicated by stitching and the thumb is separate.

The doll was called Balsam Baby because it was stuffed with balsam needles from the American fir trees.

DATE
1930
NATIONALITY
American
AVAILABILITY
rare, mid-price range
HEIGHT
16½in (42cm)

32 ART FABRIC MILLS DOLL

A miniature version of the life-sized doll made by Art Fabric Mills. Two dolls of this small size accompanied the life-sized doll on the cloth.

She has coloured lithographed hair, features, underclothes and footwear.

DATE
c1900
NATIONALITY
American
AVAILABILITY
*easy to find,
inexpensive*
HEIGHT
8in (20cm)

33 IZANNAH WALKER

Izannah Walker of Rhode Island, USA, was granted a patent for her cloth dolls in 1873, though she was producing them commercially before that date.

The method was to soak cloth in glue and to press it in a two-part mould. The dry head was then padded, covered with stockinet and re-pressed.

After the two halves had been glued together, the surface was painted with oil colours.

This moulded and painted doll has curls at the back and brushmarks in the front and is wearing black boots.

DATE
c1873
NATIONALITY
American
AVAILABILITY
rare, expensive
HEIGHT
18in (45.5cm)

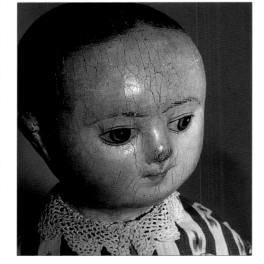

34 POPEYE

A Dean's Rag Book Popeye the Sailor man. He was a film cartoon character of the 1930s, known for his appetite for spinach, which enabled him to perform deeds of strength and daring. His example coaxed millions of reluctant youngsters to eat their green vegetables. He had a rather plain girl friend, Olive Oyl.

DATE
1930s
NATIONALITY
English
AVAILABILITY
rare, inexpensive
HEIGHT
20in (51cm)

35 MICHELE LEPINAY DOLL

Many French doll artists work in cloth. This doll by Michele Lepinay has a refreshingly naive quality which is accentuated by the almost featureless face and childlike clothes.

Lepinay's dolls were made of stuffed cotton. She made only small quantities for a period of some five or six years in the 1980s and is no longer doing so.

DATE
c1982
NATIONALITY
French
AVAILABILITY
rare, expensive
HEIGHT
23in (58cm)

36 JOHN WRIGHT DOLLS

R. John Wright Dolls Inc. is an American felt doll-making company started by John Wright and his wife, Susan, in the 1970s. Their first models with moulded faces were a series of character old men and women, in the finest tradition of Lenci, Steiff, Kathe Kruse and other doll-makers of their type. They now make children, the most popular of which are characters from children's books such as *Christopher Robin*, *Red Riding Hood* and *The Little Prince* seen in the illustration above. Two of their dolls, Arthur and Lilian, are based on the Wrights' son and daugher.

Their techniques are sophisticated, enabling them to maintain a high degree of quality and attention to detail and accessories. Both the Wrights are fully involved in all stages of the work, from making the scale drawings to the sculpting of the dolls in clay and painting the dolls' features.

DATE
1980s
NATIONALITY
American
AVAILABILITY
easy to find, inexpensive
HEIGHT
approx 18in (46cm)

36

Paper Dolls

Paper has been a necessary part of civilization since the 2nd century BC and paper toys and figures were known in Europe as early as the 15th century. In the 18th century German engravers made paper soldiers and scenes which could be put together to make a record of everyday life.

Paper dolls with dresses were not known in Europe until 1791. In her book *The Collector's Guide to Antique Paper Dolls* Clara Hallard Fawcett quotes an advertisement in the *Journal der Moden* "A new and very pretty invention is the so-called English doll which we have lately received from London. It is properly a toy for little girls but it is so pleasing and tasteful that mothers and grown women will likely also want to play with it, the more since good and bad taste in dress or coiffure can be observed and, so to speak, studied. The doll is a young female figure cut out of stout cardboard. It is about eight inches [20cm] high, has simply curled hair and is dressed in underclothing and corset. With it go six complete sets of tastefully designed dresses and head-dresses which are cut out of paper . . . The whole thing comes in a neat paper envelope which can be easily carried in a hand-bag or work-box to give amusement at parties or to children." The custom of presenting paper dolls in "a neat paper envelope" continued for many years thereafter.

Until 1798, paper was handmade. In that year, Louis Robert, a clerk in a French paper mill, invented a machine to manufacture it. The machine was introduced into England, where it was being used by 1803.

Not many dolls dated before 1810 have come to light, which is not surprising considering the delicacy of the material, and most of those early examples that have appeared have been handmade. However, in that year a London publisher named S. & J. Fuller produced some sets of cut-out dolls to go with little books of stories and poems. One of the best known of these is *The History of Little Fanny*, a story with a high moral tone accompanied by seven cut-out figures of a girl in a variety of costumes, such as a milk girl, an errand girl carrying a basket of fish and a beggar girl to illustrate the scenes in the book. In the fifth edition of the series, only the head was separate, extending down the neck to a point that fitted into the different costumes but in the fourth edition, the complete doll is shown, wearing a shift.

Boys were included in this pastime; Fanny had companions named Little Henry, Albert, Frederick and Helen. There were also paper soldiers for boys, printed by Epinal in France and later by McLoughlin of America, Tinsel pictures, which could be embellished with metal shapes and there was a Boy's Paper Dressing Doll, published in about 1850 as a companion to the one for girls.

After about 1850 many paper dolls were printed in Europe and America, but before that date they were mainly German or French. There are two early French paper dolls in the Musée des Arts Décoratifs, Paris, which must have been costly toys designed for wealthy children. Dating from the 18th century, the dolls are backed with cardboard and their dresses, covered with 18th-century fabric, are decorated with lace, silver and gold and are lined with paper. They could have been part of a theatrical production, but in any case they are interesting as two very early examples of French paper dolls.

In the 1840s, engraving was replaced by lithography and while previously paper dolls had to be hand-coloured, now they could be given large areas of bright colour very quickly. They were produced by firms of booksellers and toymakers, and as the century progressed, different fashions and innovations in paper dolls came and went. Instead of the usual tabs attaching the dresses to the doll, they were sometimes designed with a front and a back to slip over the doll's heads like real clothes.

As in the world of dolls, manufacturers were quick to discover the advertising value of a famous "personality", and paper dolls of the Empress Eugénie and the renowned singer Jenny Lind were best sellers – one version of Jenny Lind has 10 dresses and head-dresses.

The English firm of Raphael Tuck produced many novelties, one of them a baby's face with arms and a bottle which could be taken apart. There was Gibson's Roundabout doll which had a skirt that folded back to make a stand. There were embossed figures, dolls with tongues that appeared through a hole in the paper, dolls with moving eyes, moving arms and legs, with interchangeable faces and many other imaginative ideas to capture the attention of the customers.

Raphael Tuck was the foremost producer of paper dolls in the UK towards the end of the 19th century. He was born in East Prussia but emigrated to London in 1865, found work and a home and brought his wife and six children over to join him. He and his family opened a small shop selling prints and frames in Bishopsgate, London, and three years later, his company started to publish lithographs, chromographs and printed novelties, such as the "scraps" beloved of the Victorians. Tuck took out a patent for his first series of Artistic Paper Dolls in 1893 and they were a great success. His dolls range in size from 5½in (14cm) to 13in (33cm) and they are lithographed in full colour.

Among the many dolls printed by Tuck are the Fairy Tale series of Dressing dolls, The Prince and Princess series of Dressing Dolls, The Belle of Newport, The Bridal Party series, and a set of the Kings and Queens of England, but there were dozens more, too numerous to list here.

J. W. Spear & Sons was another English firm which printed paper dolls. Some were printed on thick embossed paper and it also introduced interchangeable heads, which were quite popular.

American publishers were as enthusiastic as the British about paper dolls. The firm of Kimel & Forster of New York published an interesting set of paper dolls about 1866 entitled The American Lady and her Children in a Variety of Beautiful Costumes, which included 25 changes of costume designed to be glued together at the edges and slipped over the dolls' heads.

Most famous of all was the firm of McLoughlin Brothers, which established themselves as publishers in New York in 1828. The company's first paper dolls appeared in the 1860s when it produced their General Tom Thumb and his bride, Commodore Nut and Minnie Warren. Later they made Susie Simple, Diane the Bride, Amelia and so on. Its French paper dolls featured the characters of Marie, Henri and Louise.

Advertising dolls were popular in America, a great number and variety of them being offered by McLaughlin's coffee firm (not to be confused with McLoughlin, the publishing company). They were double-sided dolls with slipover clothes. O.N.T. Spool Cotton was another firm, with advertising dolls named Amelia, Etta and Lena. There were also The Enamiline dolls, the Willimantic Thread Co. dolls and the Hood's Pills dolls, all of which probably proved irresistible to small girls out shopping with their mothers. Colgate Palmolive later used the Dionne Quins in the form of paper dolls to advertise their products.

Magazines were quick to see the possibilities of increased sales by including paper cut-out dolls on their pages. From 1908 to 1915, the *Ladies Home Journal* (USA) published a series of paper dolls drawn by Sheila Young, called the Lettie Lane series, which was followed by the Betty Bonnet series. In 1919, *Good Housekeeping* followed suit and Sheila Young invented a long-running tale about Polly Pratt and her outfits. There were also paper dolls in *The Woman's Home Companion* and the *Pictorial Review*.

Film stars were featured in the 1930s, among them Vivien Leigh in *Gone With the Wind* and, of course, Shirley Temple, the child star.

The Japanese are famous for their paper dolls, which are quite unlike anything seen in Europe. Paper was imported into Japan in the 6th century and it is possible that the first cut-out silhouettes and paper dolls were made about then. They were originally made to ward off evil and sickness, later becoming playthings and decorative objects. The Japanese have the greatest number of hobbyists in paper-folding (origami) and in paper doll-making and their paper dolls come in all shapes and sizes, to be used as wall pictures, bookmarks, greetings cards and menu decorations.

1 TINSEL PICTURE

 The tinsel portrait was really an early form of paper doll, in which theatrical or historical figures were decorated with foil trimmings and sometimes dressed in silks and satins.

The heyday of the tinsel picture was from 1810 to 1850. The foil trimmings could be bought at shops which sold the portraits or the typescripts of the plays in which the theatrical figures had acted.

This one is a picture of St Denis of France on his horse, a subject which lent itself readily to tinselling on the sword, helmet, cloak and horse accoutrements. After tinselling, the figures were cut out, mounted on a suitable background and framed.

DATE
c1820
NATIONALITY
English
AVAILABILITY
easy to find, mid-price range
HEIGHT
7½in (19cm)

2 TINSEL PICTURE II

 "Miss Scott as Fatima" is the title of this tinsel picture, in which we see Miss Scott declaiming her part in a white satin dress decorated with a variety of tinsel ornaments.

The craft of tinselling was considered mainly an occupation for boys, though girls and adults tried it too. The decorations were manufactured by a Mr J. Webb who is said to have had 5,000 different steel punches or dies for stamping out the shapes and sizes required. The foil could be bought in several colours – silver, gold, steel bronze or shiny green. The shops also sold pieces of silk, satin or velvet cut to fit the figures, but it was considered more enterprising to cut these out at home.

DATE
c1820
NATIONALITY
English
AVAILABILITY
easy to find, mid-price range
HEIGHT
7½in (19cm)

1

ST DENNIS OF FRANCE

2

MISS SCOTT as FATIMA.

3

3 LITTLE FANNY

 The London publisher S. & J. Fuller produced what seem to be the earliest paper dolls for children. *The history of Little Fanny*, was published in 1810, and was accompanied by a paper doll with a series of outfits that changed six times during the telling of the story. She had a companion named Little Henry, whose head slotted into seven different outfits, and friends named Helen, Albert and Frederick.

Fanny's costumes show her with a book, as a milk maid, as an errand girl, in her walking outfit, as a bread seller and as a beggar girl. The rhyme to go with the last outfit is:
"Can this be Fanny, once so neat and clean?
How chang'd her dress, how alter'd is her mien".
The little figures are hand-coloured.

DATE
c1810
NATIONALITY
English
AVAILABILITY
easy to find, mid-price range
HEIGHT
4in (10cm)

4 BOXED SET

An interesting set of paper dolls was published by Kimel & Forster of New York about 1866 entitled "The American Lady and her Children in a Variety of the Latest Beautiful Costumes". There were 25 changes of costume and they were glued together at the edges and slipped over the doll's head.

These three outfits show a girl skipping, skating and bowling a hoop. The set cost $1 (58p) or two for $1.50 (88p).

DATE
c1860
NATIONALITY
American
AVAILABILITY
easy to find, mid-price range
HEIGHT
4in (10cm)

5 BACK VIEW OF BOXED SET

When the backs and fronts of "The American Lady and her Children" were glued together, the dolls could stand.

The box cover, printed in English, Spanish and German, establishes that the publisher's address at the time of publication was 254 Canal Street, New York. The firm of Kimel & Forster was there until 1871.

DATE
c1860
NATIONALITY
American
AVAILABILITY
easy to find, mid-price range
HEIGHT
4in (10cm)

6 MARIE AND HENRI

Marie and Henri are from McLoughlin's (USA) series number 247, "French paper dolls in an envelope 10c". These dolls were also published in Germany in embossed sheets with the trademark "WS/B". They were also produced by Willimantic Thread Co. as advertising dolls. McLoughlin published these dolls in two sizes and there is a third doll not shown here, named Louise. Marie is 5in (12.5cm), Henri is 4in (10cm) and the small girl is 3¾in (9.5cm).

DATE
c1891
NATIONALITY
American
AVAILABILITY
easy to find, mid-price range
HEIGHT
5in (12.5cm)

7 ERDMANN CUT-OUT DOLL

A 10in (25cm) cut-out doll of high quality by Erdmann, with her wardrobe. Made by J. W. S. Bavaria, she has six hats, two dolls, a teddy bear and a dolly bag among her items of clothing. There are even hangers in the wardrobe for her dresses.

The lettering on the outer box is in French, so she must have been made for the French market. A great many paper dolls sold in France, England and the USA were, in fact, printed in Germany.

DATE
c1910
NATIONALITY
German
AVAILABILITY
easy to find, mid-price range
HEIGHT
10in (25cm)

8 DIONNE QUINS

These paper cut-out dolls of the famous Dionne Quins were published in 1940. The girls were born in 1934 and there was no end to the appearance of Annette, Cecile, Emelie, Marie and Yvonne on postcards, sheet music, magazines and, of course, paper dolls.

They appeared as a cut-out advertisement for Palmolive soap and then on this set by the Merrill Publishing Company of Chicago, USA, which also published many film star paper dolls.

DATE
1940
NATIONALITY
American
AVAILABILITY
easy to find, inexpensive
HEIGHT
8in (20cm)

9 SINDY

Young World Productions of London produced cut-out dolls in the 1970s. Here is Miss Sindy, a giant-sized doll (of 8½in, 21.5cm). The book tells the story of Sindy and her small sister, Patch, which was the copyright of Pedigree Dolls Ltd. The doll was designed to be pressed out of the front cover and it would stand supported by a cardboard strut. The photographs show the cover of the book and inside pages.

Sindy was introduced in 1963 and was one of Pedigree's star dolls. She was a 12in (30cm) teenager with hair that could be styled and many outfits to war which were updated every year and a range of accessories such as hairdryers, furniture and so on. A paper Sindy was a logical extension of the Pedigree doll.

DATE
c1970s
NATIONALITY
English
AVAILABILITY
easy to find, inexpensive
HEIGHT
8½in (21.5cm)

10 GONE WITH THE WIND

The Merrill Publishing Company of Chicago, USA, published a great many cut-out dolls, among them a Ballet Dancing Colouring book featuring Marie Taglioni and later on film stars such as Sonja Henie, the skating star, Deanna Durbin and Jane Withers. This was published in 1940 at the peak of the success of the film *Gone With the Wind*.
Printed on quite thick paper, the book gave two Rhett Butler dolls, two Scarlett O'Hara dolls, and the film star Ann Rutherford, who played Scarlett's sister in the film, was the fifth doll. There were 11 dresses and nine outfits for Scarlett and Rhett and about three or so for Ann Rutherford.

DATE
1940
NATIONALITY
American
AVAILABILITY
easy to find, inexpensive
HEIGHT
8½in (21.5cm)

11 SPEARS INTERCHANGEABLE HEADS

The firm of J. W. Spear & Sons was British, but their dolls and games were printed in Bavaria. The dolls were often printed on thick, embossed paper and were brightly coloured. Another innovation was dolls with interchangeable heads, which became quite popular, though dolls with fixed heads were also sold.
This example shows a doll with three heads and three costumes with accessories, including a feather boa. Altogether the set would have had six outfits.

DATE
1910
NATIONALITY
English
AVAILABILITY
easy to find, inexpensive
HEIGHT
9in (23cm)

12 PAPER SOLDIER I AND II

Paper and card figures of soldiers are believed to have originated from the sheets of printed uniforms and battle scenes first produced in Germany, though Strasbourg is also mentioned as the birthplace of these unusual toys. The printer Seyfried produced some paper sheets of cut-out soldiers which he sold in the streets and other printers soon took up the idea. This Prussian-looking gentleman, printed by McLoughlin about 1900, is actually wearing the dress uniform of a US soldier for the period just after the Spanish-American war.

DATE
c1900
NATIONALITY
American
AVAILABILITY
easy to find, inexpensive
HEIGHT
4in (10cm)

The other soldier, published by McLoughlin, is wearing the campaign uniform for US soldiers for the period after the Spanish-American war, when there was fighting in Cuba and the Philippines. The British were the first to use khaki uniforms during the Boer War, which was about the same period.

13 McLoughlin Doll

This doll comes from the McLoughlin Bros. book entitled *Wide World Costume Dolls* number 538 (1920). These dolls had been published previously in about 1911 in sheet form, which is why the dresses are not 1920s period.

Each page of the book contained a doll and three costumes with hats, and each costume had a name and note about it. This doll is presumably Anna, "who lives in Russia, which is a vast country across the sea. In winter Anna goes for long sleigh rides all bundled up in thick furs so she won't be cold". The other two dolls are Susan, in a tennis outfit and Jeanette, in a silk coat with lace ruffles.

DATE	*1920*
NATIONALITY	*America*
AVAILABILITY	*easy to find, inexpensive*
HEIGHT	*9in (23cm)*

13

14

14 Mary Quant Daisy Doll

The Daisy paper doll was published by Collins, London, about 1974. There were four books in the series, entitled *Daisy's Fashion Wardrobe*, described as "The only doll with real-life fashions by Mary Quant". The clothes were in scenic settings with accessories.

The doll is a typical 1970s girl, with her gingham tops and platform-soled shoes, now all looking quaintly old-fashioned.

DATE	*c1974*
NATIONALITY	*English*
AVAILABILITY	*easy to find, inexpensive*
HEIGHT	*9in (23cm)*

15 Raphael Tuck

In the year 1871 Raphael Tuck published his first Christmas card and nine years later the firm of Raphael Tuck registered its trademark, an easel and palette. Raphael Tuck was born in East Prussia, but he and his family moved to London in 1865 to escape the Prusso-Danish Danish and Austrian wars. Tuck took out a patent for the first series of "Artistic Paper Dolls" in 1893. This particular one is from the "Artistic" series number 103, which shows a fanciful collection of dresses that do not seem to fit into any known era.

DATE	*c1890*
NATIONALITY	*English*
AVAILABILITY	*easy to find, inexpensive*
HEIGHT	*5½in (14cm)*

15

16 LETTIE LANE

From October 1908 to January 1915 *Ladies' Home Journal* published a series of paper dolls which were drawn by Sheila Young. In total, there were 36 pages of these dolls.

This one, entitled "Lettie Lane Comes Home for Christmas" is the last in the series. In March 1915, Sheila Young started another series of paper dolls entitled "Betty Bonnet" and on this sheet, Lettie is "coming back to the Journal to show children her new clothes and hats and shoes, to introduce them to her new friend, Betty Bonnet, and to wish them a merry Christmas". "Betty Bonnet" continued until 1918.

Paper dolls printed in colour were not new in the USA at this time; as long ago as 1859 *Godey's Lady's Book* had published clothes for a paper doll in colour, with the figures in black and white.

DATE
1915
NATIONALITY
American
AVAILABILITY
easy to find, inexpensive
HEIGHT
6in (15cm)

16

17 FAIRY DOLL

This doll and her companion were donated to the Musée des Arts Décoratifs, Paris, in 1923. They are backed with cardboard and their dresses are lined with paper. This one has a golden halo and is holding a feather in her right hand. She has silk chenille wings and is wearing curious socks.

The style of dress is 18th century and presumably both dolls were intended to depict angels of a rather theatrical type. On the cardboard backing is a crudely bent copper wire, so they may have been suspended, perhaps as part of a crèche scene.

DATE
18th century
NATIONALITY
French
AVAILABILITY
rare, expensive
HEIGHT
11½in (29cm)

18 FAIRY DOLL II

This second very rare paper doll once also had a golden halo. The doll's features and accessories are hand-painted, and her elaborate dress of 18th-century fabric is decorated with lace and silver and gold. She is holding a red heart in one hand which, like the feather of the first doll, is clearly symbolic.

DATE
18th century
NATIONALITY
French
AVAILABILITY
rare, expensive
HEIGHT
11in (28cm)

Dollhouse Dolls

Small dolls for dollhouses have been made in most of the materials mentioned in this book, from wood and wax to celluloid and vinyl. Not all owners of dollhouses give them inhabitants, preferring to leave the rooms unoccupied, but in the past many people liked to make their doll's houses more homely by adding a family, servants and even pets. There is no doubt that they make a dollhouse more interesting from the point of view of social study.

How did our ancestors live? What sort of servants were considered necessary for the large house of a German merchant of the 17th century? What toilet arrangements were there? How was food cooked and stored? Where did everyone sleep? What heating arrangements were made? These questions could doubtless be answered without the need for dolls, but it is infinitely more interesting to see the actual family going about their daily lives, with the servants using kitchen implements, putting pans on the fire, or waiting at table wearing their fine livery. Dollhouse dolls certainly bring a dollhouse to life.

There are one or two rules for dollhouse dolls. The most important one is that the dolls should be to scale; a huge cook taking up most of the space in the kitchen destroys the illusion of reality very quickly. They should also be dressed suitably, preferably in a period style appropriate to the age of the dollhouse while a doll that is sitting down must be seen to be doing so properly, with knees bent, not just propped up against a chair.

Having said this, many of the dolls in the older houses break all the rules. Two of the oldest houses in the Germanisches Nationalmuseum in Nuremberg, Germany, dating from the 17th century, have inhabitants, which give them a wonderful feeling of life and bustle. The Kress house wax dolls are, however, dressed in 18th-century clothing, which might be a little offputting to an expert on costume, though to most of us they still seem to blend in quite well with their surroundings. The Baumler house contains not only dolls, sitting in their drawing room wearing fine dresses, but a stable with two model chestnut horses which stand feeding in their manger and a coachman whose bedroom can be seen through an open door. The store room contains a very small wax doll, almost hidden behind a table.

Many of the Dutch cabinet houses are populated by dolls. The 17th-century Petronella de la Court house in Utrecht, the Netherlands, for example, has an over-large nurse holding a child in leading reins, a mother entertaining a visitor in the lying-in room, and a beautifully made, fashionably dressed gathering of men and women who are being entertained in the painted music room. There is a servant in the kitchen, three men in their smoking den, surrounded by *objets d'art*, a man in his study and several more servants and grandly dressed members of the family on the top floor.

These dolls definitely add to the atmosphere of richness and luxury. They are all dressed in the height of fashion, the men in velvet coats with cravats, the women in silks and satins and lace. The dolls are made in wax and though the figures are rather stiff, their faces and costumes are so well observed that you feel they must have been modelled from life.

An English 17th-century dollhouse containing a delightful family of dolls is the Ann Sharp house. Ann Sharp was the god-daughter of Queen Anne but her house is not a grand affair, rather a child's plaything. The complete household is presented in wax or wood, some figures modelled only to the waist, others with cardboard hands and arms, all with their names neatly printed on slips of paper pinned to their clothing. The baby and the daugher of the house are in the upstairs nursery with Sarah Gill, "ye child's maid" who has a wooden face, while the child is made of wax to her waist and is supported by her stiff skirt. Fanny Long is "ye chambermaid" and other characters are William Rochett, "ye heir", Lady Jemima Johnson, Mrs Lemon and Mrs Hannah, "ye housekeeper".

The 18th century produced several fine dollhouses and cabinets, among them the van Amstel cabinet in The Hague, which also has a fine collection of doll's house dolls, all made of wax and well-dressed, and the Blaaw house in Haarlem, the Netherlands. In England, there are several notable inhabited doll's houses, namely Uppark, where the dolls conform to the early 18th-century convention of the servants having wooden heads and the gentry being made of wax and dressed in elegant clothes. Each lady wears the correct cap and gown and even has on the right number of petticoats. At Nostell Priory in Yorkshire there is another dollhouse with several wax and wooden occupants, and the Blackett dollhouse of the Museum of London contains two fine wax dolls.

The miniature court and town of "Mon Plaisir" at Arnstadt, Germany, boasts over 400 dolls. They are larger than usual, measuring about 10in (25cm), and they represent people from all walks of life, from shopkeepers and beggars to the prince and princess in their stately rooms, surrounded by courtiers. The dolls are made of wax and are said to have been the work of the monks at nearby Erfurt.

Wax dollhouse dolls would, of course, have been hand-made by craftsmen. It was not until the 19th century that little jointed wooden dolls could be bought ready-made for a small sum. They were made in Germany from the early part of the century, in the Grödnertal region, and exported in large numbers. The most famous group of these dolls are those owned and dressed by Queen Victoria when she was a girl of about 10, with the help of her governess, Baroness Lehzen. She has 132 of these dolls, 32 of which she dressed herself and arranged in scenes from the theatre and from court receptions. These are now in the Museum of London.

Another famous set of Grödnertal dollhouse dolls can be seen at Audley End in Essex, UK, where several of them are seated in the music room.

China-headed dollhouse dolls could also be bought in the 19th century. They usually had black hair and very white complexions. They had soft bodies which have often disappeared, leaving only the heads.

All these dolls depended on their costume for effect,

supplied either by the child or by some friendly grown-up, for in themselves they were basic little figures. By the 1880s, however, bisque-headed dollhouse dolls became the usual type of inhabitant and they were more interesting. Some had porcelain arms and legs attached to a porcelain body by wires, others had shoulder-heads on a cloth body. Some had moulded hair on a wig; others, often with the same features, were given a moustache and side whiskers and took their place as father of the household or as butler or footman.

The Hammond House at Wallington Hall, Northumberland, UK, has a fine collection of china-headed dolls of all kinds, adults and children and a full complement of domestic staff. The dolls are German, dating from about 1885 and each one is dressed in the appropriate costume of the period. An unusual feature of the Hammond House is the large number of male dolls it contains, two of which are in Scottish Highland dress.

By the 1920s the favoured material for dollhouse dolls was celluloid or composition, though in fact because they were so lightweight, celluloid miniature dolls have a tendency to fall over and are not very successful.

Dollhouse dolls of the 1990s are often made of vinyl, though doll-artists are making some extremely good-looking bisque dolls and dolls of modelling material which enables them to produce fine detail on a small scale.

Caring for dollhouse dolls

The same rules apply to cleaning small dolls as to large ones — take great care, do not soak a doll in water or cleaning fluid and always try out a small area first.

Collecting dollhouse dolls

Dollhouse dolls are less expensive than full-sized dolls, though at auction they tend to be sold in groups, which increases the overall price.

1 VAN AMSTEL HOUSE DOLLS

Early Dutch dollhouses are quite different from the realistic representations of houses familiar to us from Victorian times. They were a series of little wooden boxes placed in large wooden cabinets for the display of collectors' miniatures. Often, they were populated by wax doll figures dressed in fine clothing, like the one shown here, in the Sara Ploos van Amstel doll's cabinet in The Hague Gemeentemuseum.

The doll is seen in the garden room of the cabinet, which is decorated with perspective views of formal gardens. She is dressed in a pale blue silk dress and has a wax head and hands.

DATE
18th century
NATIONALITY
Dutch
AVAILABILITY
rare, expensive
HEIGHT
approx 5in (12.5cm)

2 DUTCH MEN

DATE
late 17th century
NATIONALITY
Dutch
AVAILABILITY
rare, expensive
HEIGHT
approx 5in (12.5cm)

Just as beautiful as the Van Amstel cabinet is the Petronella de la Court doll's cabinet in the Centraal Museum, Utrecht, which shows us in precise detail how wealthy Dutch families of the late 17th century filled their homes with precious works of art and other treasures.

The cabinet contains many doll figures, playing their parts like actors in the nursery, the lying-in room, the kitchen and here, in the painted music room, where a fashionably dressed gathering is being entertained and a game of cards is being played for money. The dolls are well-proportioned, with wax heads and hands and they all have a plentiful supply of hair.

3 ANN SHARP HOUSE DOLLS

This dollhouse, which belonged to Ann Sharp, who was god-daugher of the future Queen Anne, is another cabinet house. It is the oldest English doll's house known and it is inhabited by a delightful family of dolls. The whole household is presented in wax or wood, some modelled only to the waist, some with cardboard hands and arms. They all have their names written on slips of paper pinned to their dresses or coats.

This is Sarah Gill, "ye childe's maid" with a child and baby. Sarah is elegantly dressed for a maid, but she has a wooden head (wooden heads usually indicated servant status) and cardboard arms and hands. The child has a wax head and arms but no legs, being supported by her skirt. The baby is also wax.

DATE
late 17th century
NATIONALITY
English
AVAILABILITY
rare, expensive
HEIGHT
approx 5in (12.5cm)

4 ERIC HORNE DOLLS

These little wooden peg dolls were made by Eric Horne, a craftsman who now makes pedlar dolls and other toys, leaving the doll's house dolls to his son, Peter. Though they look a little like the old Grödnertal dolls, these are actually much simpler, with pipe cleaner arms and legs. Here we see a dairy maid, a parlour maid, a cook and, in the foreground, a clown.

DATE
c1980
NATIONALITY
English
AVAILABILITY
easy to find, inexpensive
HEIGHT
about 5in (12.5cm)

5 SIMON VAN GIJN DOLLS

The kitchen of the small dollhouse in the Simon van Gijn Museum, Dordrecht, is occupied by a wooden-headed cook, who was probably made earlier than the house itself. She is a typical 18th-century doll, with a painted face and flat, carved hands. She is wearing a fine, fancy frilled bonnet and apron as she stands by the sink in front of the water cistern. The cooking area, filled with cooking utensils and a roasing spit, is dominated by a frilled canopy, which was typical of old Dutch kitchens.

DATE
18th century
NATIONALITY
Dutch
AVAILABILITY
rare, expensive
HEIGHT
6in (15cm)

5

6 GLAZED PORCELAIN DOLL

Madame de Presle gave her dollhouse to the Musée des Arts Décoratifs, Paris, complete with family and servants. The kitchen of the house occupies a small space between the salon and the dining room, so there was not much scope for the usual fine display of cooking utensils, but the cook looks quite at home in it, with a small dog in front of the stove for company. The doll, probably German, has a glazed porcelain shoulder head and porcelain lower arms attached to cloth upper arms. She is dressed in a gown of some coarse fabric and is wearing a rough apron, both of which seem at odds with her rather charming face. The house is dated about 1850, and the doll appears to be contemporary with the house.

DATE
c1850
NATIONALITY
German
AVAILABILITY
easy to find, mid-price range
HEIGHT
approx 5in (12.5cm)

6

7 WAX-OVER DOLLS

The doll on the left has the slight crackle associated with wax-over-composition dolls; the doll on the right does not, though she too is wax. These two dolls are also inhabitants of the Madame de Presle dollhouse and are therefore dated about 1850.

DATE
c1850
NATIONALITY
possibly French
AVAILABILITY
rare, expensive
HEIGHT
approx 5in (12.5cm)

8   JILL BENETT DOLLS

These exquisitely-dressed dollhouse dolls are made by one of the leading English doll artists, Jill Bennett. Their fine modelling and the detail of their dresses makes them collectors' items.

Jill Bennett trained as a theatre designer and started to make dolls in the 1970s, using porcelain that enabled her to put in fine detail on a small scale. The dolls have porcelain hands, lower limbs and lower arms, and stuffed bodies. They all stand firmly on their feet without support.

Each doll is carefully observed and each has a different character.

DATE
1993
NATIONALITY
English
AVAILABILITY
easy to find, inexpensive
HEIGHT
5½in (14cm)

9

10   KITCHEN WORKERS

A housekeeper, two chefs and two kitchen maids are busy preparing a meal in the kitchen of one of the fine houses of "Mon Plaisir".

The dolls have wax heads and wooden or fabric bodies, and it is interesting to see how each doll is dressed for the part he or she is playing; the housekeeper is distinguished by a large white apron and a bunch of keys at her waist; the maids are prettily dressed, with caps but no aprons; the chefs wear traditional tall white hats and white clothes.

DATE
first half of 18th century
NATIONALITY
German
AVAILABILITY
rare, expensive
HEIGHT
approx 10in (25.5cm)

9   PRINCE AND PRINCESS

In the Castle Museum in Arnstadt, formerly in East Germany, is the amazing miniature world named "Mon Plaisir", which Princess Augusta Dorothea von Schwartzburg-Arnstadt created from about 1704 until her death in 1751.

Miniature scenes of the town, court and even some of the countryside, populated by over 400 dolls, are contained in 80 cases in the museum, which have miraculously been preserved since the Princess's death. This scene portrays the Princess, seated on a throne, receiving her husband, who appears quite often in different scenes wearing this yellow costume to distinguish him from the courtiers, who wear red.

DATE
first half of 18th century
NATIONALITY
German
AVAILABILITY
rare, expensive
HEIGHT
10in (25cm)

10

11 MUSICIANS

A delightful quartet of musicians can be seen in the painted music room of "Mon Plaisir". The wax-headed gentlemen all have full-bottomed wigs and red French-style coats decorated with gold braid. The wax-headed girl is reading an aria, to be accompanied by unfamiliar instruments which resemble a lute, an oboe and a form of piano. The scene has such a convincing air of reality about it that it was probably observed from life.

Two monks from nearby Erfurt made most of the wax heads and hands of the models, whose bodies are made of wood or fabric. The costumes were made by girls in the neighbourhood.

DATE
first half of 18th century
NATIONALITY
German
AVAILABILITY
rare, expensive
HEIGHT
approx 10in (25.5cm)

12 KING'S LYNN DOLLS

A modern doll in old-fashioned dress from the King's Lynn dollhouse. The façade of this dollhouse (c1740) is a copy of the house at 27 King Street, King's Lynn, UK, which belonged to a Dutch merchant named Flierden. He used some of the rooms as offices. The dollhouse was made for his daughter, Ann.

The dollhouse had to be completely restored in 1984, when it was given a set of modern dolls in 18th-century costume. This bisque porcelain doll, representing Mr Flierden in his counting house, was made by the doll artist Jill Bennett.

DATE
1984
NATIONALITY
English
AVAILABILITY
easy to find, inexpensive
HEIGHT
approx 5½in (14cm)

11

12

13 GLAZED PORCELAIN DOLLS

A glazed china dollhouse doll with delicate bisque lower limbs, a cloth body, painted features, black hair and wearing her original clothes. An interesting feature of the doll is that she has two left hands. She is wearing blue painted boots with flat soles, three petticoats (one flannel) and lace-trimmed, tucked pantalettes.

DATE
c1830
NATIONALITY
German
AVAILABILITY
easy to find, inexpensive
HEIGHT
6in (15cm)

Index

BIBLIOGRAPHY

Anderton, *Twentieth Century Dolls* (Wallace Homestead, 1971).

D.B.&E. Coleman, *The Collector's Encyclopaedia of Dolls* (Robert Hale, 1986).

Betty Cadbury, *Playthings Past* (David & Charles, 1976).

Leslie Daiken, *Children's Toys Throughout The Ages* (Spring Books).

Nora Earnshaw, *Collecting Dolls* (Collin's, 1987).

Clara Hallard Fawcett, *The Collectors' Guide to Antique Paper Dolls* (Dover, 1987).

Antonia Fraser, *A History of Toys* (Weidenfeld & Nicolson, 1966).

Fritzsch & Bachmann, *An Illustrated History of Toys* (Abbey Library, 1966).

Brenda Gerwat-Clark, *The Collector's Book of Dolls* (Quintet, 1987).

Caroline G. Goodfellow, *Understanding Dolls* (Antique Collectors' Club, 1983).

Vivien Greene, *English Dolls' Houses* (Batsford).

Mary Hillier, *The History of Wax Dolls* (Souvenir, 1986).

F. G. Jacobs, *A History of Dolls Houses* (Scribner).

Constance Eileen King, *The Collectors' History of Dolls* (Robert Hale, 1977).

Constance Eileen King, *Antique Toys and Dolls* (Studio Vista, 1979).

William C. Ketchun, Jr, *Toys and Games* (Cooper-Hewitt Museum, 1981).

Opie, *The Treasures of Childhood* (Pavilion, 1989).

Pollocks History of English Dolls and Toys, K. & M. Fawdry (Ernest Bonn, 1979).

Pollocks Dictionary of Dolls, Mary Hillier, ed. (Robert Hale, 1982).

M. & V. Seeley, *How to Collect French Bébé Dolls* (H.P. Books, 1986).

Maree Tarnowska, *Fashion Dolls* (Souvenir, 1986).

Max von Boehn, *Dolls* (reprint) (Dover, 1972).

Gwen White, *European and American Dolls* (Batsford, 1974).

PICTURE CREDITS

r = right   l = left   c = centre   t = top   b = bottom

Abbey House Museum, Leeds, UK: p16 *(b.l)*, *(c.l)*, p36 *(b)*, p97 *(b.r)*

Author's Collection: p130 *(c.l)*, *(c.r)*

Bath Costume Museum, Bath, UK: p118 *(b.r)*

Beryl Collins Collection: p35 *(b)*, p39 *(b.r)*, p48 *(b.l)*, p50 *(t)*, p52 *(b)*, p54 *(r)*, p84 *(l)*, p86 *(l)*, p90 *(b)*, p93 *(b.r)*, p95 *(r)*, p96 *(t)*, p103, p104 *(r)*, p108 *(b.r)*, p109, p110, p111 *(t.l)*, p113 *(l)*, p118 *(b.l)*, p125 *(t)*, *(b.l)*, p141 *(b.r)*

Castle Museum, Arnstadt, Germany: p140 *(c)*, *(b)*, p141 *(t)*

Centraal Museum, Utrecht, The Netherlands: p138 *(b.l)*

Charlotte Zeepvat Collection: p112

Coleman Collection: p25 *(b.r)*, p47 *(b)*, p64 *(t.r)*, *(c.r)*, *(b.r)*, p98 *(b.r)*, p105 *(t.l)*, p107 *(t.r)*, p108 *(c.r)*, p126 *(l)*, *(t.r)*, p135 *(t)*

Collection de Galea, Musée National de Monaco: p18 *(b.r)*, p22 *(t)*, p23 *(b.r)*, p72 *(r)*, p78 *(t)*, p79 *(b)*, p84 *(b.r)*

Collection Haags Gemeentemuseum, The Hague, The Netherlands: p41 *(c)*, p48 *(t.l)*, p96 *(b)*, p138 *(t.r)*

Edinburgh Museum of Childhood, UK: p17 *(t.l)*, p19 *(b.l)*, p77 *(b.l)*, p81 *(t.r)*, p82 *(c)*, p97 *(l)*, *(t.r)*

Harry Rinker Collection: p25 *(l)*, *(t.r)*, p49 *(r)*, p54 *(c.l)*, p98 *(l)*

Hove Museum and Art Gallery, UK: p20, p29 *(t.r)*, *(b.r)*

Key Desmonde Collection: p30 *(b)*, p88, p121 *(t.r)*

Legoland, Copenhagen, Denmark: p65

Lilliput Museum, Isle of Wight, UK: p21 *(t)*, p23 *(b.l)*, p24 *(b.r)*, p33 *(l)*, p38 *(b.l)*, p40 *(b)*, p43 *(b)*, p53 *(c.r)*, *(b.r)*, p62, p68 *(t.r)*, p81 *(b.r)*, p91 *(b.l)*, *(b.r)*, p92, p93 *(l)*, *(t.r)*, p94, p95 *(l)*, p99 *(c.l)*, p104 *(l)*, p105 *(t.r)*, *(b)*, p106, p107 *(l)*, *(b.r)*, p108 *(l)*, p118 *(t)*, p119 *(r)*, p123 *(r)*, *(b.r)*, 124 *(b.l)*, *(t.r)*, p127 *(t.l)*, p132 *(t.r)*

London Toy and Model Museum: p28 *(t.l)*, p75 *(t.r)*, p102 *(l)*, p120 *(l)*, p121 *(l)*

Lynton Gardiner: p127 *(b)*

Marion Jennings Collection: p130 *(b.l)*, p131, p132 *(b)*, p133 *(t)*, *(b.l)*, p134 *(t)*, *(b)*

Mildred D Seeley Collection: p80 *(b)*

Mrs Wolters von Bummel, The Netherlands: p89 *(b,l)*

Musée de Jouet, Poissy, France: p47 *(t)*, p67 *(t.l)*, p75 *(l)*, p77 *(b.r)*, p78 *(b)*, p79 *(t)*, p80 *(t)*, *(c)* p85 *(l)*

Musée des Art Decoratifs, Paris: p22 *(b)*, p56 *(r)*, p57, p126 *(t.r)*, p135 *(b)*, p139 *(r)*

Museum of Childhood at the Judges' Lodgings, Lancaster, UK: p28 *(b.l)*, p39 *(t)*, p47 *(c)*, p81 *(l)*

Museum of Childhood, Ribchester, UK: p50 *(b)*, p66 *(t)*, p68 *(b.r)*, p119 *(b.l)*, p122

Museum of London, London, UK: p31 *(b)*

Museum Simon van Gijn Dordrecht, The Netherlands: p23 *(t.r)*, p37 *(l)*, p46 *(b)*, p83 *(b)*, p117 *(b.r)*, p139 *(b.l)*

Netherlands Kostuummuseum, The Hague, The Netherlands: p24 *(l)*

Overbeck Museum, Devon, UK: p76

Penrhyn Castle, Gwynedd, UK: p41 *(b)*, p83 *(c.l)*, p120 *(b.r)*

Polly Edge: p85 *(t.r)*, p87 *(t.r)*, p125 *(b.r)*

Private Collection: p29 *(l)*, p30 *(t)*, p32 *(b)*, p40 *(t)*, p87 *(b.r)*, p124 *(b.r)*, p140 *(t)*

Sonneberg Spielzeug Museum, Germany: p16 *(c.l)*, *(t.r)*

Stranger's Hall, Norwich, UK: p18 *(b.l)*, p48 *(b.l)*, p60 *(t)*

Strong Museum, New York, USA: p102 *(r)*

Sudbury Hall, Suffolk, UK: p21 *(b)*, p39 *(l)*, p91 *(t)*

The late Z. Frances Walker Collection: p64 *(c.l)*, p126 *(b.r)*

Tunbridge Wells Museum, Kent, UK: p39 *(t.r)*, p40 *(c)*

By courtesy of the Board of Trustees of the Victoria & Albert Museum: p32 *(t)*, p37 *(t.r)*, p73 *(t.r)*, p86 *(b.r)*, p87 *(l)*

Wardown Museum, Luton, UK: p41 *(t)*

Warwick Museum, Warwick, UK: p66 *(b)*